RAISING
DRUG
ADDICTS

RAISING DRUG ADDICTS

A Father's Account, with Lessons Learned
and Sections by my Daughter
from the Orange County Jail.

*It is only by the grace of God I
am alive to tell this story!*

Robert Mitchell
with
Hannah Mitchell

WESTBOW®
PRESS
A DIVISION OF THOMAS NELSON
& ZONDERVAN

WestBow Press books may be ordered through booksellers or by contacting:

WestBow Press
A Division of Thomas Nelson & Zondervan
1663 Liberty Drive
Bloomington, IN 47403
www.westbowpress.com
1 (866) 928-1240

ISBN: 978-1-4908-8197-3 (sc)
ISBN: 978-1-4908-8199-7 (hc)
ISBN: 978-1-4908-8198-0 (e)

Library of Congress Control Number: 2015908338

Print information available on the last page.

WestBow Press rev. date: 6/8/2015

TABLE OF CONTENTS

FOREWORD

By Pastor Lisa Cram of the Prelude Foundation

Notifying someone of the unexpected death of a loved one is probably the hardest thing I will ever be called on to do as a Pastor. You cannot change the situation: Platitudes and religious ideology do not provide complete comfort no matter how strong your faith; You cannot say that you understand unless you've had an identical experience; and you cannot make the pain stop. You really don't have any answers and the ones your natural mind may think of are not acceptable. The reality is, all you can do is to simply be there, being available.

This family's story is one of tragedy and victory. As I read it, I laughed and I cried and I remembered...

Once upon a time I was Hannah. And if you have lived a dysfunctional life in some way, then so were you. Perhaps not Hannah but Christian or Bobby. Or maybe you'll see your issues revealed through the eyes of the parents. The point is, the details of our stories vary but we are all strongly connected through our mutual imperfections, chaotic experiences and missteps.

I've been free from the bondage of alcohol and incarceration for 32 years now. Even still, I have "issues". Don't you? We all do; there will always be something in our character and quality to overcome. This book is a beautiful opportunity to be reminded through another's point of view, of the frailties that can so easily shatter our ability to choose wisely.

Bondage is debilitating, whether to drugs or money, in handcuffs or otherwise. There are many ways to be afflicted. The beauty of our Savior, Jesus Christ, is that we can choose freedom at any point along the way. And delivery is free!

I'm confident that no matter what your own tale may be, you'll find a lot to relate to in this book. It's life. It's messy. The journey isn't always fun; to the contrary. But when we LET God in, we can be sure that it will be Good. And if we can manage to arrive at that divine place of "count it all joy" (James 1:2-4), then wow! Meanwhile…

The difference between dysfunction and a healthy life is choice. The path to getting there is decision. The ability to stay the course is focus.

Consider this: what you are 'looking' at has a hold on you. For now, have a look inside…

PREFACE

I am certain that raising drug addicts is not what most parents expect to do when they have children. To the contrary, I am sure that most parents expect their kids to be president of the greatest nation on earth, just as my wife and I did. Ok, maybe not quite president, but most of us have high expectations for our children. However, never in my life would I have thought I would raise even one drug addict, let alone three out of three.

This is a true story; one that I have written with sections by my daughter during her time in the Orange County Women's Jail. My goal is to help anyone who has or plans to have kids, or anyone who is dealing with a loved one who has or is suspected of a having a substance abuse problem. I started this book on my own, before my daughter was arrested and pleaded guilty to charges related to substance abuse. Later, it made perfect sense to ask her to write about that part of her life.

I did not write this story to embarrass any of my children, who, for whatever reason, decided to explore the darker side of life for a time. All of my children approved of me writing the book in a fully transparent manner, and they share my vision of helping others in this process.

This experience played out in Southern California between the cities of Ventura and San Diego. When I started writing the book, we were an upper middle class Caucasian family of five. Substance abuse does not discriminate. By the time I was halfway finished with the book, we were and are, a family of four as my middle child, Christian, who was only twenty-six at the time, died, ultimately, because of drug and alcohol addiction.

My oldest child, Bobby, started abusing drugs around 1996. He has been free of addiction for thirteen years.

I started writing the book in February of 2014 after a few of my employees jokingly told me I should write a book. I replied, "yes, I will call it Raising Drug Addicts." I was only half-serious at the time but they encouraged me to get started on the book. The story continues to evolve as you read on.

My daughter, Hannah, began writing her sections while she was still in jail and finished shortly after her release. She is now out of jail, working her way back to a normal life, drug free, and free from the bondage of drug addiction and all that comes with it.

One thing I have learned over the past sixteen years is that law is far more complicated than we may think, and criminals typically do not realize how complex it is or how fast their crimes can escalate from something that seems to be just one small act, to a mass of felonies.

If you are using drugs or addicted to drugs or alcohol but haven't yet been in trouble with the law, with friends, with family, or with your health, thank God and stop using NOW!

If you have already progressed beyond experimenting with drugs, get help! This book is not really meant to target current drug addicts who have already sunk so deep that a book won't help them, but it may help loved ones get them the help they need. It is never too late to stop until it kills you!

If you are reading this because you are now struggling with a loved one who is abusing or addicted to drugs or alcohol, or if you suspect someone you love is addicted but you cannot confirm it, this book is for you. You can learn from my experiences, and I hope the book is helpful. I pray that my pain and suffering, and that of my children, can benefit others.

If you have any questions I didn't answer in the book, but feel I might have answers for, please write to me at raisingdrugaddicts@gmail.com or find us at raisingdrugaddicts.com.

DEDICATION

*"Commit your way to the Lord, Trust also in Him,
And He shall bring it to pass. He shall bring forth your
righteousness as the light, and your justice as the noonday."*

—Psalm 37:5-6 (NKJV)

I dedicate this book to my son, Christian, and all the parents, children, and spouses of those who have, or are currently abusing drugs or alcohol. You are the unsung heroes! Those who have not walked in your shoes cannot feel your pain.

I also want to thank my son, Bobby; his wife, Bethany; and my daughter, Hannah, for allowing me to write this book so transparently, with the desire to help others, even though telling their stories could be embarrassing for them. I started writing *Raising Drug Addicts* before Christian passed away, and he welcomed the idea of me using his history and his name in this book.

I also want to thank Hannah for prayerfully proofreading each chapter and assigning the opening scriptures from the Orange County Women's Jail. I want to give credit to Hannah for her sections on her life in jail and afterward, and most importantly, for her allowing our Lord and Savior Jesus Christ to love her, as He placed her in jail (not unlike the Apostle Paul) where He could reach her and save her life both physically and spiritually. Hannah became a woman of God during her incarceration and I am proud that she is my daughter.

I want to thank my dear wife, Angie, for allowing me to write this book. I know it hurts to read such details about our kids, but Angie shares my vision of reaching people who are enduring the journey we have been through and are seeking help or want a book they can give their children to read before they take the wrong path in life or simply before it is too late to intervene.

I want to thank all of my employers, past and present, many of whom are friends, who have hiked this trail with us.

Lastly, I want to thank our pastors for all their support, love, and prayers these past sixteen years.

I want to thank Pastor Brett Peterson and Pastor Chris Fowler, and my brothers and sisters at Living Water Community Church for their prayers and support.

I want to thank Hannah's Pastor, Lisa Cram, from the Orange County Jail, for her service. It was Lisa whom our Lord used to lead Hannah to Him.

Chapter 1

AMERICA'S CANCER

"For my life is spent with grief, And my years with sighing; My strength fails because of my iniquity, And my bones waste away. I am among a reproach among all my enemies, But especially among my neighbors, and am repulsive to my acquaintances; Those who see me outside flee from me."

—Psalm 31:10–11 (NKJV)

In the beginning was God. God created humanity, humanity created drugs, and Satan uses them to kill and destroy families and wage war on this nation and most others!

Drug addiction in America is a cancer. It is eating away at the very foundation of this great nation: the family! Perhaps I am closer to this problem than most and thus biased in my belief, but when I read the statistics, I am confident I am correct.

In Orange County, California, a bedroom community primarily made up of middle-class Christians, Jews, Buddhists, and Muslims, some estimate that one in three boys over the age of sixteen is currently using heroin on a regular basis. Take a quick glance at the DEA table below and you can see the alarming drug abuse trends in the United States. The once-feared heroin has had a stable to increasing market for years, mostly because of the proliferation of opiate-based prescription pain relievers. Another drug that has been increasingly abused year after year for decades

1

is methamphetamine (meth). Both heroin and meth are relatively cheap drugs compared to the former drug of choice, cocaine.

DEA Domestic Drug Seizures					
Calendar Year	Cocaine (kgs)	Heroin (kgs)	Marijuana (kgs)	Meth (kgs)	Hallucinogens (dosage units)
2013	22,512	965	267,957	3990	116,215
2012	36,694	999	388,059	4,622	870,203
2011	32,374	1,075	575,960	2,485	3,954,732
2010	30,053	713	725,858	2,188	2,604,797
2009	50,704	618	671,650	2,007	3,422,593
2008	50,461	605	662,137	1,518	9,311,715
2007	98,065	623	360,708	1,112	5,677,739
2006	71,604	816	328,275	1,804	3,745,560
2005	118,128	622	283,382	2,161	8,868,465
2004	117,844	669	266,088	1,656	2,196,988
2003	73,720	788	254,242	1,680	3,038,916
2002	63,513	709	238,646	1,347	11,824,798
2001	59,415	747	272,120	1,634	13,863,756
2000*	58,674	546	331,964	1,771	29,293,957
1999	36,163	351	338,247	1,489	1,717,305
1998	34,447	370	262,180	1,203	1,139,524
1997	28,674	399	215,348	1147	1,099,825
1996	44,735	320	192,059	751	1,719,239
1995	45,309	876	219,830	876	2,768,046
1994	75,031	490	157,181	769	1,368,437
1993	55,528	616	143,055	560	2,714,575
1992	69,322	722	201,483	352	1,308,018
1991	67,016	1,174	98,593	289	1,294,273
1990	57,021	535	127,792	272	2,832,084
1989	94,939	758	286,371	896	13,125,011
1988	60,951	728	347,305	694	10,467,864
1987	49,666	512	629,839	198	6,556,891
1986	29,369	278	490,607	234	4,146,711
Source: DEA (STRIDE)					
*CY 2000 had several large LSD seizures					

If you are old enough to remember the sixties and seventies, you might be wondering how this increase in heroin use could occur. Most of us who remember those decades saw the effects of heroin and therefore have difficulty understanding how anyone could even consider using that drug. The answer to the question – "why would anyone use heroin" can be found at your local pharmacy. As one becomes dependent on opiates, the receptors in the brain become less responsive to the previous levels of opiate being taken. This causes the brain to desire more than just maintaining a feeling of being normal.

Most friends and loved ones of the opiate addict have difficulty observing any outward signs of addiction since taking the opiate makes the addict seem normal, unlike a person under the influence of other types of drugs, like marijuana or LSD.

As the dosage level needed increases, so do the withdrawal effects, which get worse as the dependency grows. In the end, the addict will either have a very painful withdrawal process or will eventually die from an overdose or suicide. It is a narrow trail with few turns. There are just these three paths to the end.

At the time of this writing, the National Institute on Drug Abuse estimated that "alcohol, and illicit drugs is costly to U.S., exacting over $428 billion annually in costs related to crime, lost work productivity, and healthcare." In 2013, the institute's survey results indicated that "1 in 15 people who take non-medical prescription pain relievers will try heroin within 10 years." This is exactly what happened to my middle child, Christian. First he became addicted to the prescription pain relievers he was given for a broken foot. When he found it too difficult to renew his prescription for painkillers, his "friends" hooked him up with heroin. Our first clue was finding a burnt spoon on our patio when we returned from vacation in 2008. We never confirmed it was Christian's, but I knew what I was looking at. He said he had some friends over, and the spoon must have been one of theirs. We believed him!

The saddest part of drug addiction, in my opinion, is the fact that much of the money spent on heroin, meth, cocaine, and marijuana is funneled back to groups like Al Qaeda, ISIS, and the Taliban, who then use the profits to fund their wars against the United States and other free nations. In other words, the abusers in the free nations are financing the terrorist wars against their own countries, even funding the beheading of Christians and Jews. I only wish the users could see it this way. I have asked many drug users if they realize this point, and they always look at me like deer in headlights. They just haven't thought it through, and once addicted, they can't!

People often ask if more dangerous drug use starts with marijuana. I cannot say that the addiction of my children to more dangerous drugs is the effect of starting with marijuana, and I am not sure the scientists can say that marijuana use causes one to crave something stronger. Personally, I don't believe there is a cause-and-effect relationship between using marijuana and craving stronger drugs. Most likely, people see marijuana as a starting point to experimentation since it is so commonly considered an innocent drug, less dangerous than alcohol. What I can say is that every drug addict I've ever talked to said he or she started with alcohol, then progressed to marijuana, and then moved on to stronger drugs. I can also say, marijuana is addictive. Many will disagree but many a marijuana addict will attest to this addiction. I know two at my fitness center who have failed every attempt to stop using marijuana.

With the flood of prescription painkillers all around us, however, the correlation between marijuana and more powerful drugs may be changing. It seems innocent enough to try one of Mom's or Dad's back-pain pills. After all, "they come in a bottle with a prescription from a doctor," one addict told me. He went on to say, "My mom's pills don't come wrapped up in a piece of foil." There are plenty of painkiller addicts who say they never smoked marijuana but became addicted to opiate-based painkillers and moved on to the cheaper version, heroin, when the money got tight or their doctors quit writing prescriptions.

The other drug that has been on the rise for decades is methamphetamine. It is a relatively cheap drug to buy, and it is easily manufactured from the back of a truck in a remote location. The signs of meth abuse are more obvious than those of heroin. The meth addict most often loses weight rapidly; has frequent mood swings, including acting out in violence; has acne-like sores; is often very jittery and talkative; and doesn't sleep or sleeps for days at a time when he or she comes off the drug. Meth addicts often have feelings like something is crawling on them. They can stand in front of a mirror for hours, looking at themselves and picking at their skin. Long-term use will likely result in deterioration of the teeth, brain seizures, strokes, and aneurisms. Like heroin, meth is highly addictive.

Meth addiction occurs as the drug increases dopamine production, which results in high levels of dopamine in the brain. Dopamine is related to feelings of motivation, pleasure, motor function, and reward. Meth's ability to release dopamine rapidly in reward regions of the brain produces the feeling of euphoria. Long-term meth use (and some studies indicate short-term use as well) actually alters the brain, and some studies have reported this brain alteration can be permanent, which makes it even more difficult for the meth addict to withdraw and remain meth free. In meth withdrawal, the addict first becomes depressed and loses his or her ability to experience pleasure as the dopamine levels drop. This can occur over a period of thirty to ninety days. After the initial withdrawal, the craving for more methamphetamine begins. It is relatively common for suicide to be the end of this phase. It is estimated that more than 90 percent of meth addicts return to abusing the drug during the withdrawal phase if they don't commit suicide. Like any addiction, meth withdrawal is not only difficult, but it is also quite painful, just as heroin withdrawal is.

In The Wall Street Journal, on August 18, 2014, writers, Gary Fields and John R Emshwiller reported:

> "Over the past 20 years, authorities have made more than a quarter of a billion arrests, the Federal Bureau of Investigation estimates. As a result, the FBI currently has 77.7 million individuals on file in its master criminal

database—or nearly one out of every three American adults."

They didn't break these arrests down by violation, but anyone who sits in a courtroom, even for one day, will see that the majority of arraignments involve illegal drug use and driving under the influence of alcohol.

I asked Hannah, my daughter, what most people seem to be incarcerated for, and her response was, "Probably eighty percent of all inmates are in jail [like her] for drug abuse or alcohol abuse related crimes." It's a sad state of affairs in the U.S. and most other nations, so I ask myself, "where is this war on drugs," we occasionally hear of in the news?

Lessons Learned

If you are prescribed a drug, get to know the drug. Do your own research. Don't rely strictly upon your doctor or pharmacist to tell you how the drug will affect you. The Internet has all the resources you need to find this information—its right at your fingertips.

If you are using any medications that others might want to experiment with, lock them up!

Never trust a substance abuser. Do your own research and get to know what's happening to you if either you or your loved one is a user.

There is a war against the free world by organizations that want to annihilate those who disagree with their views. This war is very much funded by drug addiction. The money spent by a drug user can come back to the United States or other free nations in the form of a human bomb or perhaps even worse.

If you find that your kitchen spoons are missing or turning up burnt, you have a drug problem in your house.

Chapter 2

STICKING TOGETHER

"Then the rib which the Lord God had taken from
man He made into a woman, and He brought her
to the man. And Adam said: This is now bone of
my bones And flesh of my flesh; She shall be called
Woman, Because she was taken out of Man. Therefore
a man shall leave his father and mother and be joined
to his wife, and they shall become one flesh."

—Genesis 2:22–24 NKJV

This is the most important chapter in the book. If you are the loved one of a substance abuser, I know your pain. All the issues that come with substance abuse are difficult to deal with, whether you were abused intentionally or whether you're simply the passive victim of an abuser in your family. Parents, children, and spouses all suffer. In his book, *Limitless Life*, Derwin L. Gray says,

> In some ways, addiction is like a tornado. The addict's life
> is flung around a like a rag doll. His or her families and
> friends are battered and beaten emotionally, sucked dry
> financially, and many times physically beaten as well.[1]

---

[1]   *Limitless Life* by Derwin L Gray is a Nelson Publication.

He goes on to say,

> Addiction is a black hole that sucks in everyone touched by it. The "addict" label is ruthless. The plague of addiction has been especially cruel to my family, holding an entire generation at gunpoint and abducting their potential.[2]

Derwin could not have better described the impact addiction has on a family. To my wife, Angie, and me, it has been like a prison sentence that just won't end. As I write this book, we are sixteen years into this sentence, and we pray a parole day will soon come into view. In the meantime, we seek the glory of our heavenly Father in every event we endure. If we cannot glorify God, our experiences are a waste.

If you are one of the abused, I pray you are not alone in your quest for healing. After all Angie and I have been through I don't know how either of us could have survived without each other; our friends at church; our pastors; and most importantly, the love, mercy, and grace of our Father and Creator.

If you are trying to survive the consequences of a family member's substance abuse on your own—don't! Realize and remember that first of all, we were created to be dependent because we were created incomplete. The key to a peaceful life is to understand that we were designed to be dependent first on Him, our Creator, and then on one another in the body of Christ. So join a support group or get help in your church, your synagogue, or elsewhere—but get help! You will likely need to talk through your experiences at some point with others who can simply listen.

Angie says I will talk to anyone about anything I am going through. That's because I find it not only therapeutic, but also a ministry for me. Because I often get to share my faith, I've been able to help some abusers along my journey.

---

[2]   Ibid.

In my last job, I walked two miles during nearly every lunch break, and some of my team members would join me. At times, I may have been too graphic in describing to them some of the details of our issues with our kids, like Hannah's experiences in jail. I hope I wasn't.

Back in 2003, I had my oldest son taken to the hospital because I was afraid he would injure or kill himself while he was on crystal meth. While I thought I had done the right thing, my wife thought I was so completely wrong that she threatened to divorce me. There was so much verbal fighting in our house and occasionally some shoving between my son and me that Angie had had all she could take. Seeing her son taken away in the back of a police car had just been too much for her, and in her mind, I was to blame. I always wondered, however, exactly what she was blaming me for.

It has been said many times that people are often cruelest to those they are closest to. When dealing with a drug-abusing child, spouses often blame each other for the problems in their homes. Courtrooms are filled with divorce cases over the drug abuse of couples' children. It's a sad state in America and most other freedom-loving nations.

Angie and I have been devout Christians since 1981. Divorce is not common in the churches we attend, and the Bible clearly teaches that divorce is not God's will.

As difficult as it was for me to imagine life without Angie, I said to her, "Okay, if that is what you want, let's go to the self-help divorce court and do it ourselves instead of spending money on attorneys." Financially, the attorneys always win in divorce court; we would have needed every dollar we had just to be able to separate and start our lives over.

We attended a self-help night, and the attorney we met with couldn't figure out why we were there. She suggested we take the paperwork home and think about whether we really wanted to divorce. Although the issues with our kids are still unresolved, we have stuck together for thirty-two years of marriage. Angie still has that paperwork, though. I know she has held on to it for many years, but I think it's just because it got stuffed in a corner … at least, I hope that's why!

Neither of us spends much time thinking, *Why me?* or *Why us?* We just pray for each other, pray for our kids, and keep moving forward. If we didn't have each other and our faith, I'm not sure where we would be right now. I do know that most marriages that experience what we have been through end prematurely. However, we are still making it through our difficulties together.

Job 2:9 says, "Then his wife said to him, 'Do you still hold fast to your integrity? Curse God and die!'" Job endured more than Angie and I could ever imagine, and yet he maintained his integrity in spite of the advice of his spouse. If you and your spouse are experiencing a family member's substance abuse and each of you sees the situation differently, seek impartial counseling and commit to getting through it together. If you have made a commitment to serving Jesus Christ, you will make it through as one.

Lessons Learned

If you are going through what Angie and I have been through, you cannot do it on your own! As Christians, we have our faith in our Lord, Jesus Christ, and we have had each other all along. I would not be alive today if it were not for my faith and my wife. If you are not in this with someone close to you, find a support group.

Don't give up! Fight the good fight and get counseling if you find this cancer is tearing at your relationships. If you don't attend a church, find one and you will find a good counselor.

Pray for yourself and for the substance abuser in your life. Never give up! Look for the positive in every event.

Expect the abuser to attempt to manipulate you and to attempt to create divisions between you and others who are in this with you!

Keep yourself in good shape. Exercise frequently to burn off some of the stress!

Chapter 3

IN THE BEGINNING

"And if it seems evil to you to serve the Lord,
choose for yourselves this day whom you will serve,
whether the gods which your fathers served that
were on the other side of the river, or the gods of
the Amorites, in whose land you dwell. But as for
me and my house, we will serve the LORD."

—Joshua 24:15 NKJV

This story begins in Thousand Oaks, California, which is in southern California between Los Angeles and Santa Barbara.

I was born in a small town in Kansas, but for all but three months of my childhood, I was raised in Thousand Oaks. Growing up in this small town in a valley covered with California oaks was like living in *Little House on the Prairie*. In fact, that series was actually filmed just a few miles north of Thousand Oaks. *Gunsmoke* was filmed less than two miles from my house, and we played in the abandoned movie sets as kids. We were surrounded by the incredible outdoors, and as a young boy, I enjoyed every minute of it. As I look back, it is difficult to believe, even for me, how we lived. During my first week of kindergarten, my mom walked a mile with me to school, along with two other mothers walking their own kids. After that first mile, however, we were on our own. That might be considered child endangerment these days. As the populations of small towns across the United States have increased, so too have crime rates and the number of criminals, along with the issues that stem from them and their impact on innocent lives.

When I was young, in the 1970s, there was a big problem with heroin, as there is now. For nearly thirty years, it seemed to have been all but eradicated. By the late seventies, however, most people my age wouldn't even talk about heroin because it was so obvious that it was destroying the country. Marijuana use, on the other hand, was everywhere. By the time I was in high school, it seemed like everyone except me was using pot, including several of my high school teachers.

I admit that I was different. I thought about smoking pot with my friends, but I had a feeling that it would hurt my parents if they found out, so I just didn't experiment with drugs—at least, not until I was twenty-three years old and in school doing prelaw. I got some pot from a friend, took it to the garage, and tried to smoke it. By that age, peer pressure didn't affect me much; it was just an experiment for me. I knew I would never smoke pot recreationally, but I wanted to see what all the hype was about. Fortunately, I couldn't manage to inhale it—otherwise, my life may have been ruined from that day on.

I met Angie in Thousand Oaks in the fall of 1979, and we married in 1981. I was a technician at Rockwell International at the time and made a decent lower-middle-class income. Angie was an accounting clerk for a capacitor manufacturer.

Angie and I were quite involved in church and I was attending seminary. We planned to be a traditional family when we started having kids. Back then, traditional meant that she would stay at home and raise our children. We were going to have the perfect family.

Our first child, Bobby, was born in June of 1985. Shortly afterward, we moved to a small ranch house in Simi Valley, California, just a few miles north of Thousand Oaks. At the same time, I was promoted to my first salaried, white-collar position. This was a lot of change to take on at one time and it was quite stressful.

Angie resigned her job, as we had planned, and stayed home to tend to our newborn little man. We continued to attend church and serve in leadership roles, however. We thought then and still think now that this is the way a family should be. Angie worked in the church nursery and I headed the New Believers ministry.

Even though being a traditional family meant sacrificing a good chunk of our income, we got by even with our hefty mortgage. We were anything but monetarily rich, but we were rich with love, and we loved our son. We enjoyed the simpler parts of life. Our weekly treat was a blended iced coffee on Friday night at Gloria Jean's, a specialty coffee shop in the Thousand Oaks Mall. We would walk through the mall with Bobby to my favorite pet store where we would pet the parrots as we sipped our coffee. We would have had to save for a month for enough to go to the local drive-in movie theater, and since we could never afford to pay for a babysitter, anyway, Bobby went everywhere with us.

Nearly three years later, Angie got pregnant again, just as we had planned. The next nine months went by without a hitch, and she gave birth to our second son, Christian. As Christian grew older, Bobby had a best friend. They did everything together. I have many fond memories of Bobby placing his arm around Christian's neck or resting it on his shoulder and escorting him outside to ride his tricycle, play in the dirt, or just go out on the patio and play with our dog, Pluto (whom Bobby had named).

Christian was easy to raise in his early years. He hated to get in trouble and had a tender heart. Bobby was more resistant—I won't say, "Rebellious"—to mentoring in his younger years.

The photo above was taken in our ranch house when Bobby and Christian were approximately six and three years old.

Having two children was our goal, so we figured we were finished having kids, even though I wanted a girl more than ever. We debated for a few years about which of us should do something permanent about not having any more kids, and then, one day, Angie broke the news to me. "I am pregnant," she said. I prayed for a girl, and on March 19, 1991, Hannah was born. She came when our Lord decided it was time for us to have the girl I had always wanted.

This picture of Christian and Hannah was taken when they were
about five and two years old. All three of our kids cherished each
other and were good friends, which is unusual for siblings.

In June 1995, I was offered a job in South Orange County with a big
pay increase. I accepted the position, and we moved to a place called

Trabuco Canyon, where we still live today. I wanted to raise my kids in the outdoors, as I had been raised when I was a young boy growing up in Thousand Oaks. Trabuco Canyon was perfect! The kids were young, so the move was not too difficult. As much as we love Trabuco Canyon and though we have the best neighbors you could imagine, Simi Valley remains our other home; our fondest memories are of life in that little ranch house.

In a flash, we moved from our humble beginnings to an upper-middle-class neighborhood full of people with money and some pretty unruly kids. We went from not being able to put our boys in Boy Scouts because we couldn't afford the uniforms to joining as soon as we got settled in our new home. We tried the boys in sports, but the only sports they seemed to like were soccer and dirt bike riding.

Life in Orange County seemed pretty normal for our kids. They had plenty of friends and appeared to adjust to the relocation. I have many fond memories of Boy Scouts, backpacking, camping, and just being with my boys as they grew up. If we weren't on an outing with the Scouts, we were dirt bike riding or just camping at O'Neal Park by our home.

Hannah settled in more easily than the boys. I believe it was because she was only four years old when we moved. When she got older, she joined the Brownies (the female version of the Cub Scouts), and later, she became a Girl Scout. I love my kids. I remember Hannah trying out for cheerleading in Long Beach, California, when she was about eight years old. Her daddy got tears in his eyes seeing how fast his daughter was growing up.

I still remember my neighbor Joel and I suiting up and taking our little girls to the Girl Scouts' father–daughter dance. I cherish the memories of my time with Hannah. We all truly loved the place where we lived. Our lives were not flawless, even though we lived the good life, but they were far from disastrous.

By the time Bobby was twelve years old, however, we had begun to experience issues with him. When he was sixteen, we strongly suspected he was using marijuana. Now, you're probably thinking, *What was your first clue?* Well, finding a marijuana plant at the side of our house was a pretty solid clue.

As I reflect on the past sixteen years of our family history, I believe that, up to this point, life had been pretty normal. I have done some research on the word *normal*, but I wasn't impressed with the definition I found, as it doesn't fit in with this book. Statisticians have a formal definition of the word normal, however: "a bell curve of normally distributed outputs from a stable system of inputs." Using this definition, we can describe the normal behavior of our loved ones as "consistent over time." In other words, normal means not observing any significant behavioral changes.

In Bobby's case, although we started to observe some changes which obviously concerned us, for the most part, his behavior (the outputs of his system) remained consistent. He was still riding dirt bikes, racing BMX, fishing with his brother and his friends, coming home at night as required, making consistently good grades in school, and just being a pleasant, polite, and respectful kid. Bobby successfully completed all the work required to earn the rank of Eagle Scout, which ninety-nine percent of Boy Scouts never achieve.

At this point in our lives, we had not seen any behavioral changes in Hannah or Christian, so our life as a family remained normal.

Unfortunately, though, in March of 2002, I lost my job due to a plant shutdown when the economy was in bad shape. We had to move in order to keep the money coming in. At this time, Bobby was sixteen, Christian was thirteen, and Hannah was ten.

Lessons Learned

Enjoy the simple life in the ranch house and never miss a day telling your spouse and your children that you love them.

Be observant of subtle changes in interests, friends, attitude, appearance, and school grades, or if items of value seem to disappear.

If you are considering moving your children away from their comfortable surroundings and friends, consider the risks carefully.

Watch your kids closely and start screening their friends at an early age so they will be used to it.

Chapter 4

GROWING PAINS

"I, therefore, the prisoner of the Lord, beseech
you to walk worthy of the calling with which you
were called, with lowliness and gentleness, with
longsuffering, bearing with one another in love."

—Ephesians 4:1–2 NLT

With the plant shutdown in Orange County, I was given six months' notice to find a new job. Despite the poor economy, one of my former employees gave me a solid lead, and surprisingly, it was back in Thousand Oaks where I had grown up. I tend to look for God's hand in everything, and it seemed He was in charge of this move and preparing our hearts to return to our roots.

I interviewed for a position in charge of corporate audits but instead was offered a position in charge of lean operations under a world-renowned quality executive. Things seemed to be lining up. The job came with everything a company could offer, including money and events to help the kids meet new friends and settle in. As I look back, the only problem was the fact that we had to sell our home in Orange County and buy again in the Thousand Oaks area within six months, or lose our relocation money. So we sold and bought again, which turned out to be our first big mistake.

We bought a former model home in a really nice area of Simi Valley called Wood Ranch. It was a planned community with the best schools and good neighborhoods. Hannah was in the sixth grade, and her school was right behind our new home. Christian was a freshman in high school, and Bobby was a senior.

At this point, some of you might be hearing alarm bells going off inside your heads. Yes, those are the wrong ages to move most kids. All three of ours were well established in Orange County, and moving them away from their friends and the home they had lived in for the past seven years turned out to be quite devastating. It was easiest for Hannah, probably because she was the youngest. She made new friends, played soccer, and really enjoyed the Boys and Girls Club of Simi Valley. We settled in at a new church and Angie and I made some new friends as well.

Christian resumed Boy Scouts. He was the top kid in the little troop he joined in Simi. After earning his Eagle Scout rank, he stayed with the Boy Scouts another year and earned three palms, another high and rare achievement. Most kids leave as soon as they earn their Eagle rank, if they even make it that far.

In Simi Valley, Bobby started out in a regular high school and began making friends. He made one special friend whom he and his new friends nicknamed "Cheddar Bob." Cheddar was a nice young man and eight years older than Bobby, though he was slow for his age. For Bobby, he became not only a friend, but also a sort of counselor, as Bobby struggled with high school and other issues during our second year back in Simi.

Bobby owned an old GMC pickup which he, Christian, and I built into what is called a "pro street" truck. This was a big project. Bobby and his mom bought a new motocross bike as well, which Bobby rode mostly with his new friends. I had a bike too, but I sold it since I had no time to ride it, what with my new job.

Looking back at our life in Simi Valley at that point (we'd been back about a year), I ask myself, "Was life still normal for the Mitchell family?" It seemed so, but year two was coming.

Bobby seemed to have developed a short temper. He often walked to his uncle's house a few miles away and didn't come home for a while. When he was home, he seemed to be changing in a lot of ways. I started to find beer cans along the side of our house and in other places. I remember going to our community pool to check on him one time. He and Christian were in the Jacuzzi. When I got close to them, I noticed full cans of beer under the water and in the drain. Of course, Bobby and Christian didn't know anything about the beer, and I was supposed to believe that.

One day, I was placing mouse poison in our attic because we had been hearing little feet running around the ceiling. I was shocked to find a live marijuana plant in a pot (potted pot) in the attic above Christian's bedroom closet. Bobby claimed he didn't know anything about it. One thing every reader needs to know right now is this: every drug abuser or alcoholic is a liar, even to the point of being a sociopathic liar. Mark my words, if you are dealing with an abuser, you are dealing with an expert liar. Abusers start by lying to themselves about their addiction as they struggle to come to grips with the fact that they are addicted. Don't believe anything they say, because, most likely, it's all lies.

The pot plant went down the garbage disposal. I have to admit that I had known the plant was up there before I supposedly "found" it. My son will never know that I knew unless he reads this book.

If you are suffering the trials of living with a drug abuser or an alcoholic, try to find those rare opportunities to have fun with the experience. This probably sounds odd, so let me explain. Because I had known the plant was in the attic, I created the story about the pitter-patter of little mouse feet just so I could pop my head up there. When Bobby saw me climbing out of the attic crawl space in the master bedroom, he became very interested in how far I might go into that crawl space. He offered to help, but I told him I could handle it. Bobby tried harder to be helpful that day than I can ever remember him. He came up with every reason imaginable why he should place the mouse poison in the ceiling instead of me. But I insisted that I should do it because I didn't want my son to be exposed to the poison.

When I folded my ladder and started carrying it toward Christian's closet, Bobby all but came unglued. I was enjoying this, so I took my time setting up the ladder and slowly climbed it while telling Bobby how much I appreciated his concern for me and his desire to help. I opened the attic door, placed the flashlight on the ceiling, popped my head into the attic, and found the pot plant. Not surprisingly, Bobby insisted that it was not his plant and that, of course, he knew nothing about it, so the plant must all be Christian's doing. After all, I'd found it in Christian's attic. This was probably the first solid sign that at least one of our children was beginning to lose the normal life. Even though Angie and I were not drug users, this was the point at which drugs began controlling our lives.

Friendly Homeless People

Early in our second year back in Simi, we seemed to go through what we called an "event" with Bobby weekly. One day, Angie and I were pulling into our local gas station to get gas when a homeless man approached our Infiniti, looked in the window, turned, and walked away. Both of us thought his behavior was odd, and we had each independently noticed that some of the locals who hung out at the gas station were attracted to our car. *Oh, well,* we thought. *They must think we're someone else.* Not long after this, we pulled in to get gas again, but Hannah was with us this time. As one of the guys approached the car, Hannah blurted out, "That's Barry!" Angie and I were shocked to learn that our little girl knew this man by his first name. Hannah realized she had let the cat out of the bag and tried to change the subject. Eventually, however, she confessed that she knew Barry because Bobby routinely picked him up in the Infiniti when he was supposed to be taking Hannah to the Boys and Girls Club, or soccer, or a friend's house. It turned out that Bobby picked up some of these guys on a regular basis to take them to a liquor store and give them money to buy him beer.

We suspended Bobby's use of the car, but that didn't last long. I've always believed that Angie was too soft with the kids, but that is just my opinion. Perhaps if she hadn't been soft, things would have been worse. Maybe they would have started stealing cars like a lot of other kids do. At any rate, like a lot of other parents in our situation, Angie began struggling to believe the multitude of lies, and thus, she became an enabler. While Bobby was suspended from using the car and had to walk everywhere, I also worked closely with the local police to prevent Bobby's friends from buying him beer. We dried up his network, and I was glad that we did.

Before long however, we were into our next major event. After about four weeks, Bobby was back to driving the Infiniti. About 5:00 p.m. one Saturday, we received a call from a Simi Valley police officer who politely told us, "If you come right now, you can pick up your car and save the impound fees." We jumped into my Nissan Sentra and drove to the place he said we would find our car. It turned out that Bobby had been teaching a fourteen-year-old girl (his friend's sister) to drive the Infiniti, and she had nearly hit a mailbox.

Although we grounded him again, he was back to the driving again within a few weeks.

I Knew It When the Doorbell Rang

One morning, at about 1:15 a.m., we heard Bobby come in, climb the stairs, and go to bed. A few minutes later, the doorbell rang. I got up, went to the bedroom door, and yelled, "Hold on, I have to put on my pants and I will be right down." While I was getting dressed, I told Angie, "Bobby has been home for fifteen minutes, so it has to be the police." I was right. Bobby had just done a beer run on the other end of town. Simi is a long valley with three main roads that run the length of it. Bobby had done his beer run eight miles away in an area known as the Knolls, which is also where Charles Manson hid from the police.

Bobby had run at least eight stoplights and exceeded ninety miles an hour in running from the police that night. They had backed off and let him go home because they figured if they continued the pursuit, he might kill himself or someone else. Bobby came down the stairs and, of course, tried to convince the police that he wasn't the one they were chasing, but they weren't buying it. I explained to one officer that I had been working with his department to dry up Bobby's beer-buying network, though apparently, burglarizing liquor stores was the result. "You may not even know about this project," I said, "so I may be giving away a secret."

The officer commented that he did know about it and went outside to make some phone calls. When he came back inside, he told me to take Bobby to get the case of beer he had dumped and then take it back to the store. Then I should take the car keys away from him and call it a night. "I am a dad," he said. I was relieved that Bobby wasn't going to jail for several felonies. Obviously, I had become an enabler as well.

Cheddar Bob Goes to See His Family

Bobby and Cheddar Bob became the best of friends. Cheddar was there for Bobby during some depressing and challenging times as he tried to cope with moving in his late teens. One weekend, Cheddar, who lived with an ailing uncle, went up north for a long weekend to see his family in Sacramento. On Saturday evening, Angie and I received a call from Cheddar. He was looking for Bobby, who wasn't home, so Angie spoke with him. Cheddar's uncle in Simi had gotten sick and Cheddar needed to return a few days early. He wanted to see if Bobby could pick him up Sunday at 3:00 p.m. at the local train station. I remember Angie telling him, "Of course, sweetie, we will have Bobby pick you up. No problem."

Bobby went to the train station on Sunday as planned and waited for the train. The train came and left, but Cheddar wasn't on it. Bobby turned when he heard someone calling out his name—it was Cheddar's uncle. He knew Bobby quite well. He said brokenly, "Bobby, Cheddar is dead! He was killed along with my brother several hours ago in a car accident." Cheddar's other, deceased uncle had been a California Highway Patrolman. After all his years patrolling California highways, his life came to an end on a local freeway as he and Cheddar were hit by a jackknifed big rig.

Bobby called home, and I answered the phone. He was emotionally destroyed as he tried to tell me what he had just heard. I offered to come up and drive him home, but he eventually regained enough control to talk to me and was able to drive home on his own. Up to that point in my life, I had never encountered anyone so devastated. If you think back to the definition of *normal*, this was an "input" to Bobby's life that was life-changing—not only for Bobby, but also for anyone close to him. We had already experienced some issues with him, but his normal behavior changed almost overnight at this very sensitive and vulnerable moment in his tender life.

Bobby still is a very nice person. He is fun-loving, a bit of a jokester, and one of the most loyal friends anyone could have. He would truly lay down his life for another person.

Normal Begins to Shift

Experts say that sudden changes in the behavior, interests, or performance (or grades) of a loved one are indicative of a major change to his or her causal makeup. Often, this causal input is substance abuse. Don't be afraid to confront it. We became suspicious of Bobby's friends. Previously, the two hobbies Bobby was fixated on were his truck project and riding his motorcycle, but after the death of Cheddar Bob, he completely lost interest in both of these hobbies, as if they had never existed. I remember a time when Christian and I were home working on Bobby's motor. Bobby got dropped off by a friend, walked through the garage, and didn't seem to even care what Christian and I were doing. It was like a light came on for me at that moment. I knew he was changing. His personality had changed a little so far, but not a significant amount. Within a month, however, his life spiraled out of control. He often didn't come home at night and never had believable explanations for what he may have been doing. He seemed to be a completely different person.

The Arcade

Late one Saturday night, after Bobby had been home for a few days, he talked Angie into letting him take the Infiniti to a local arcade to play video games. There, he parked on the white line that defined a parking space and a security guard told him to move his car so that it was within the space. A girl he was meeting there jumped into the driver's seat and said, "Let me do it. I have a driver's license." So Bobby climbed into the passenger seat and let her back the car up. He immediately discovered, however, that she couldn't drive, because she nearly backed into a Corvette. So, from the passenger seat, Bobby shoved the stick into drive and they drove the car right through the front of the arcade! Fortunately, the arcade was at the top of a stair. A curb slowed the car and prevented it from fully penetrating the crowded building. One girl got a cut on her knee, but otherwise—miraculously—no one was seriously injured.

Once we had our Infiniti in the repair shop, our insurance company said they would not insure the accident since Bobby hadn't been the one driving. According to the police report, though, the car had surged forward because Bobby had shoved it into drive, so technically, the accident was Bobby's fault, which made the accident insurable. Lawsuits began piling in, and Angie and I were left completely out of the discussions. In the end, we paid our deductible and learned that in California and most other states, liability for a car follows the registered owner whether the driver is insured or not. Keep this in mind if you have an at-risk family member driving a car registered in your name.

Nanny the Enabler

With Angie and I committed to no longer loaning our car to any of our children, Angie's mother and "the saint" (the patriarch of Angie's side of the family) bought Bobby a new Toyota Tacoma pickup. In spite of the enabling that came with this little truck, Bobby believes that it probably helped save his life, as it kept him from riding a street bike or driving his 700-horsepower project truck. The Tacoma, however, gave Bobby unlimited freedom to do whatever he wanted, anytime he wanted.

Bobby was quickly losing weight and muscle. He had once been about 220 pounds of solid muscle (a serious bodybuilder), but by this point, he was rapidly shrinking and looking ill. Often, he wouldn't come home for days, sometimes a week. He could barely hold a job, but since he had a boss who repeatedly covered for him, he was able to hang on to his current job as he shrank to nearly nothing and became easily irritated and even violent.

Sometimes, Christian and I would drive around town looking for Bobby's pickup and checking the neighborhoods we knew he frequented. We networked with his sober friends, who said that Bobby was addicted to crystal meth and alcohol. With this network, we could check on him, but trying to force him to come home did no good. The police just advised us to make sure he was safe, arguing that if they arrested him, he would be more exposed to drugs in jail than he was on the streets.

One night, Christian and I hid in some bushes under the living-room window of someone's apartment, watching Bobby, listening, and taking notes as he and some others talked about some drug dealers. We wrote their names down, and Angie and I looked for them on the weekends. Since this was a war for the life of our son, we were committed to winning. And so, we wanted to find out who the drug dealers were. Sometimes we were wrong and went after the wrong people. Nonetheless, we went to their homes and sometimes used force to get to them because they would hide when they saw us at the door. We even threatened to kill them if we ever had evidence they were giving or selling drugs to our son. Since we weren't dealing with cartels, just lowlifes, I felt comfortable that we were not putting ourselves at any serious risk. Since we had already dried up the beer-buying network, we thought we might dry up another one—the drug-dealing market!

Even though Bobby's drug addiction was short-lived, we learned a few things:

1. Never give drug addicts money.
2. Never give them gift cards, because they will sell them for pennies on the dollar.
3. Try to keep them from getting money, and try to make sure they don't submit to higher levels of crime as a result.
4. Everything drug addicts do, they do with the goal of obtaining the substance they are addicted to.

Reaching Bottom

Many have said that addicts won't seek help until they reach bottom. Bobby bottomed out and, like many in the same situation, thought that the only way out of his misery was to take his life. Angie and I were more afraid for him now than we had ever been. We didn't know what do. We had committed his ordeals to prayer and looked to God for direction all along. I even discussed the current situation with the police, who told us to take him to a hospital where he could be supervised for a couple of days and then released with some medication to help him to cope.

A few weeks later, Bobby came home from work one night and told us he was leaving for Arizona to live near his best friend, Dustin, whom he had grown up with. Dustin was clean; he had never used drugs. Bobby had just turned eighteen. Bobby was a smart kid and he knew that if he left his new friends and moved to an unfamiliar place, he could get off the drugs and have a chance at life. Today, he says, "If I hadn't left California and my friends, I would have died."

After settling in Arizona, Bobby got married and had three sons. Four years later, he and his wife separated, and Bobby and the boys moved back to Orange County. He has since married a woman from Orange County where they currently reside. Bobby is an incredible father, son, and stand-in father to Hannah's son, Noah. He had some bad years, but he has certainly made up for them. He loves his boys and Noah more than anyone could imagine. They and his new wife are his entire life!

Much like seeking fun in the midst of disaster, I like to look for the positive in all the messes. Although Angie and I have been through some very difficult years with Bobby, I can see how his past is guiding him in raising his boys. He is far from overprotective, but he is cautious about his kids' friends, and he is deeply involved in his sons' lives. In fact, Bobby is the biggest kid in his entire apartment complex! All the young kids hang out with him and the boys. They build bicycle jumps together, and Bobby rides the bikes and jumps along with them. Bobby's boys are turning into three fine young men.

Starting Over

While Bobby was still in Arizona, Angie and I pushed on with a job search to get us back to Orange County. I mentioned earlier that Christian had never really settled down in Simi Valley. He was very withdrawn, and going through two years of Bobby's drug addiction right along with the rest of the family didn't help him any. Hannah was actually more settled than Christian, but she was okay with moving back to the old neighborhood as long as we lived in the Mission Viejo School District so she could go to Mission High.

In December 2004, I was offered a job in North Orange County with a fairly significant pay increase. It was the perfect job for me, and it put Hannah and Christian back in their old neighborhood. For the first six months, I lived in Palm Springs during the week, working at our manufacturing facility, and I came home to Simi on the weekends. In February, we moved the family back to South County and bought a house less than half a mile from the home we had left two years earlier.

So, we were back home and everything was going to be normal, right? But what would normal look like? In our minds, it meant that Christian and Hannah would be as happy and content as they had been when we'd first left Orange County.

Back in South County

Christian learned that he could finish high school in adult-education home school. He only had to finish his senior year. Hannah wanted to go to Mission Viejo High. She was starting as a midsophomore. They both enrolled and were off and running, but both soon discovered that the requirements in Orange County were much more stringent than they were in Ventura County. Christian finished high school, but Hannah started ditching and hanging out with the seniors.

It wasn't long before Christian's personality and interests began to change. We recognized the pattern. His friends were his old buddies from his elementary school years in Orange County.

Christian routinely came in at night appearing to be under the influence of something, but we just couldn't figure out what. When we challenged him about it, he got hateful and cried that we didn't trust him. This was very unusual (non-normal) for Christian. He had never been a mean or an angry person—just the opposite.

One night, after we'd challenged him, he disappeared. I jumped on a bicycle and rode around for hours trying to find him. Even though he was on foot, I couldn't find him. Years later, he told us he had passed out in the drain behind our house. It turned out that most of Christian's old friends had become drug addicts in the two years we were away.

One Event After Another

When Hannah was fourteen, she ran away for an evening. We looked all over but couldn't find her. Later, we learned that she and a girlfriend had hid in a toddler park and smoked weed until they'd passed out. Another night when she didn't come home, we found her under the influence in some friend's house. Bobby, Angie, and I nearly kicked the door down to get to Hannah. We ran upstairs, pushing and shoving people out of our way, picked her up, and rushed out of the house. A parent in the house was completely shocked at what was happening. Yet another night, the police were involved. They found Hannah and held her until Angie and I could pick her up. I told the police about her drug issues and asked what we could do. "Can I tie her up at our house?" I asked. The police advised us that this was not a legal option.

Hannah's behavior when she became addicted was more obvious than Christian's; she became aggressive while Christian was usually passive— although on one occasion, he did exhibit defensive anger when we challenged him.

Hannah ended up dropping out of high school, but she completed her GED with no problem. Christian was taking business classes at Saddleback Community College. We limped along and our lives seemed to be returning to normal, but they were still not completely right.

One Saturday in 2009, Angie and I were out shopping. Before we arrived home, Hannah tipped us off that Christian was shaking and vomiting uncontrollably. When we arrived home, we comforted him and asked what was wrong. He confessed that he was addicted to heroin and was trying to get off it, but he was suffering from withdrawal. We took him to the emergency room where the doctors stabilized him and put him on medication to help him withdraw.

Christian kept more to himself than either Bobby or Hannah did. If we wanted to know anything about Christian, we had to pry it out of him. He seemed to be doing fine and always declared that he was clean and free from any drugs. Even when he got hurt in a few motorcycle accidents and one car accident, he was always cautious to warn doctors that he could not take opiate-based painkillers, no matter how bad the pain was.

Christian always lived with us, and he and I were best friends. After the withdrawals, he stayed close to home most of the time, and together, we restored antique motorcycles, reloaded ammunition, camped, fished, and blew up fireworks in the desert. Life was normal for both of us. Christian enjoyed cooking with his mom and spending one-on-one time with her.

Some parents say a girl is more difficult to raise than a boy. Many times, that seemed to be true with Hannah. When she was sixteen, she met a young man and "fell in love" with him. He was four years older than her. We didn't know about this, of course, or we would have attempted to intervene.

With drug abuse comes other abuses. Although Hannah eventually married the man of her dreams, she would frequently move back in with us for short periods. This became such a routine that she began to lie about where she was staying when she decided not to go home. I hesitate when I say "decided" because meth addicts tend to sleep for days whenever and wherever they crash—this is not necessarily the result of a decision.

When it comes to addressing the lies of a substance abuser, the abuser always has the upper hand over his or her loved ones, who naturally want to believe the abuser's lies because it is comforting to do so. The alternative is not to believe anything they say, and taking this path only stimulates confrontation with an abuser who is most likely easily irritated.

One night, we were having an exceptionally difficult time with Hannah's attitude, so we decided to drug test her. When she realized we were serious, she had no choice but to take the test, so she acted like she was proud to do it and guaranteed that it would be negative. She even offered to go to the store and buy the test with her own money. She was hoping we might think, "Well, we must be wrong," and back off, but she was wrong this time. Nonetheless, she bought the test and continued with the charade. When she tested positive for meth, as the photo below shows, she said, "It must be a false positive." By this time, however, she had already left our house, and we were talking to her on the phone.

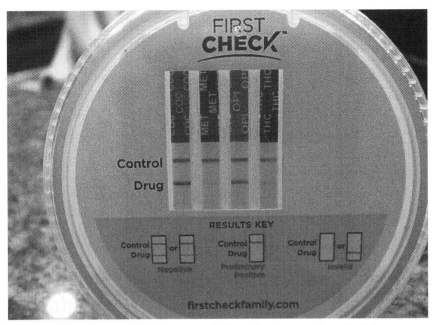

You can purchase a variety of over-the-counter drug-screening tools at most local pharmacies. The one Hannah chose is called First Check and covers four specific drugs. It includes an initial test the user performs on the spot, and it can be sent to a lab for testing at no extra charge. The results are available within a week or two.

Hannah continued to use drugs and moved back and forth for several years. Eventually, she got pregnant with her little boy, Noah. Hannah was able to stay clean during her entire pregnancy, so she knew that once she decided to get off the drugs, she could beat them if she committed to doing so.

But then, in 2014, Hannah was arrested and charged with six counts. After three months in jail, she plea-bargained to a year in jail in order to reunify with Noah. In California, if a child is taken from his or her parents and the parent doesn't reunify with the child within a court-assigned time frame, any child born later will automatically be taken from the parent at birth, regardless of the parent's status. Hannah's court-assigned time was six months, so she had no choice but to plead guilty, be good in jail and, with good time, get out in six months.

Angie and I became Noah's foster parents during the time Hannah was in jail, plus an additional several months while she worked through a multitude of requirements in order to reunify with him. Angie and I were parenting a little boy once again, and we loved almost every minute of it.

Now that Hannah is clean and thinking clearly, when she looks back, she can see the chain reaction that occurs with drug addiction and drug abuse. There is the high while you're on the drugs, followed by depression, sickness, and anger during the down side, withdrawal that sometimes results in uncontrollable fits of anger, and then, the craving for more, and more, and more. It makes me wonder why, knowing about this, people would even experiment with such drugs!

In the middle of this cycle lies the pain and suffering of loved ones, shattered lives, brokenness, and sometimes, worst of all, the little ones who get caught in the middle of it. When Angie and I went through what was required for us to qualify as Noah's foster parents, we observed this worst effect. There were many little ones under the county's protection, awaiting foster parents.

Even though Noah is our grandson and we would do anything for any of our grandsons, we were treated just like anyone else who wanted to be a foster parent—and for good reason. All the requirements were for the child's protection. We had to go to for special fingerprinting. We had to attend classes on foster parenting. Our home had to be inspected by Child Protective Services. At one point, we had to buy a baby crib within four hours. We had to sign a contract, and we had to submit to monthly and random drop-in inspections by Noah's assigned Child Protective Services Agent.

While we were going through this process, we had to meet at the county location where children were taken when they were removed from their parents. In one two-hour wait, I observed two babies—they appeared to be newborns—being checked into the facility. They had been taken from their parents, apparently at birth.

Addiction is a disease. Once you are addicted to any of the more popular drugs, namely meth, heroin, and cocaine, it becomes nearly impossible to cease using them. It's a perfect world for the drug dealers and cartels.

Addiction creeps up on its prey like a coyote in the night. No one ever says, "I am going start using this drug and then get addicted!" On the contrary, addiction starts with a thought process that includes, "I'll just do it once," followed by, "I am not addicted," and "I can do it again …" In the end, the addict realizes he or she has been caught in the snare of an evil world filled with shockingly evil people ready to capitalize on their new recruit.

Lessons Learned

All substance abusers are liars! Because you love them, you will tend to believe them. Just know this and be cautious.

Don't become an enabler. If you do, you are contributing to the addiction.

When an addict's interests change, then attitudes change, performance changes, and physical appearance even changes, because a change in the addict's personality "inputs" has occurred. Find out what those inputs are!

Never take a day for granted.

If it seems the police are tailing or "harassing" your loved one, it's most likely they know or suspect something about your loved one that you don't yet know.

Loving someone doesn't necessitate enabling them to abuse!

Getting off and staying off drugs means severing all connections to all drugs abusers.

End relationships with the addict's friends permanently.

Drug addicts will steal from anyone. Be observant for the loss of jewelry, china, collectables—anything that can be easily pawned for pennies on the dollar. Even your wedding rings are not off limits for addicts in need of their fix.

Chapter 5

SEVEN COUNTS, THE LEGAL PROCESS

"Be sober, be vigilant; because your adversary
the devil walks about like a roaring Lion,
seeking whom he may devour."

—1 Peter 5:8 NKJV

Substance abuse can ruin any occasion. At approximately 10:00 a.m. on Saturday, March 30, 2014, the morning of Bobby's marriage to Bethany, Angie received a call informing her that Hannah had been involved in a car accident. "Hannah is okay," the caller said, "but her car is hung up on a retaining wall." Hearing Angie's distressed voice, the caller again assured Angie that Hannah had not been not injured.

Committed to no longer allowing drug abuse to run our lives, Angie dressed Noah in his little tux, and Noah and I headed to Bobby's place for photos with Bobby, Christian, and the rest of the groomsmen. Angie drove to the scene of the car accident and attempted to speak with Hannah, but police were everywhere, yelling at Angie, "Get in your car and leave, *now*!"

Angie left and drove back to our house to prepare for the wedding. We had a good time at Bobby and Bethany's wedding. It was a beautiful wedding filled with love. Looking at the pictures, I can tell that Christian had a really good time as well. During the reception, Angie's cousin Julia, who owns a legal business, checked on Hannah and discovered that she had been booked on six felony counts, including one attempted murder charge, which was dropped a few days later. Apparently she had been in a fight. Of course, none of this made any sense to us, as we didn't know the whole story—and we likely still don't—but one thing we knew for certain was that this was very serious! But, continuing with the theme of fun amidst chaos, we enjoyed the reception, refusing to allow drug abuse to ruin that special, God-ordained day.

Drugs take control of everyone's life, not just the user's. Angie and I have been through this now for sixteen years, half of our married life. By then, we had learned how the legal system works, so we didn't expect to hear from Hannah for about twenty-four hours.

Three days went by, however, before she could call us, and the news was breathtaking. I tried to compare it to past experiences. Both of my parents and Angie's mom had died of slow, difficult illnesses. In a way, the news that each had passed had not been bad news, but a relief, because we knew their pain was over and that they were in heaven. Still, the news of our parents' passing was the worst thing Angie or I had ever experienced—until we got this call from Hannah. Our little girl was in serious trouble and we had no idea how to help. I believe this helplessness is the worst feeling a parent can ever endure.

A few days later, six felony charges and an outstanding misdemeanor hit-and-run were filed against Hannah. One of the felony charges included trying to hit someone with her car, even though the police had never interviewed that person. If this confuses you, don't let it. It is all about negotiation on the part of the prosecutor. The courts and the jail systems are so overcrowded that it is best for everyone if they can negotiate and avoid a lengthy trial.

If you are reading this book and you are a substance abuser, pay close attention. Chances are that you will not have your day in court in front of a jury of your peers. In California and, likely, in most other states, prosecutors will badger your attorney until you agree to confess to something and serve some time, rather than going through a long, drawn-out hearing. Hannah could have faced an additional six to ten years in prison if she'd been convicted in a trial, but a plea bargain often reduces the sentence dramatically. In addition to jail time, all the classes Hannah would have to attend, and the community service she would have to serve, a felony conviction would automatically revoke her voting privileges, her driving privileges, and her right to ever own a firearm.

Although others had also been arrested along with Hannah, the prosecutor dropped all charges against the others in exchange for their testimony against Hannah. Why Hannah and not the others, I will never know, since the case didn't go to trial, but it doesn't matter now. Hannah had made a lot of really bad decisions. She was facing the consequences of those decisions and will for the remainder of her life, be branded a felon.

After three months in jail, her feet shackled and her hands cuffed every time she was transported to court, the prosecutor made Hannah an offer she had no choice but to accept, as time was running out for her reunifying with Noah.

She was sentenced to one year in the Orange County jail. Her driving privileges were suspended for five to forty-five years, and she received five years' probation, one full year of batterers' classes, nine months of parenting classes, alcohol and drug abuse classes, alcoholics anonymous, several drug and alcohol tests each week, and community service. On top of all this, we had to pay a significant tuition for each program, and Hannah was billed $10,000 for her probation.

If a convict has a solid family with money to spare, he or she might have a chance at life after jail. Otherwise, release from jail is simply the initiation of time between jail periods for most. This is why they say, "Once in the system, you are always in the system."

Should Hannah not be able to reunify with Noah, Angie and I would pursue the process of adoption. By pleading guilty, Hannah was guaranteed a one-year sentence, a plan to be released in six months on good behavior, and a few months to work through the process of reunifying with her son.

As I write this chapter, Hannah is now fifty-five days from release. I must say that her four months in jail have been a good experience for her. She has learned a lot and has had a long time to reflect on her failures, bad decisions, and plans for the future. Jail time is a little like the military, as you will read in Hannah's chapters toward the end of this book.

While incarcerated, Hannah has committed her life to serving the Lord, Jesus Christ, and she thinks she would like to attend Bible College and minister to abused women and drug abusers. I pray that she stays the course.

Lessons Learned

What might seem simple never is when it comes to the legal system. Criminal behavior escalates faster than anyone can conceive. I, for example, would have never known that the age of a battery victim can add years to the perpetrator's sentence.

Stay out of the system. If you are reading this and you are a law breaker, stop before it is too late. Learn from Hannah's experience.

Know your rights and respectfully ensure that they are protected and respected by the authorities.

Chapter 6

JUNE 18, 2014

"For you have delivered my soul from death, My eyes from tears, And my feet from falling. I will walk before the Lord in the land of the living. I believed, therefore I spoke, and I am greatly afflicted."

—Psalm 116:8–10 NKJV

This is Christian doing what he loved most—fishing. He was truly a fisher of men.

This is the final chapter on my son Christian's experience with substance abuse. It was a difficult chapter to write, and I pray no other father has to experience its contents. I wrote it in graphic detail, hoping that the loved one of an abuser might get his or her abuser to read it.

In December 2013, Christian exited the toll road close to our home, turned onto our main Parkway, and was immediately pulled over by the police because his license plate light was broken. He had been rear-ended two days earlier, and the back of his car was pretty beaten up. He was a month away from turning twenty-six years old. He had been driving for ten years and never received a citation. Angie had always said, "He drives like an old lady."

The officer asked him if he had been drinking, a standard question for any young person pulled over in South Orange County. Christian answered truthfully, "Yes, a few beers up to three hours ago, but I am okay." The officer then asked him to step out of the car and take a sobriety test.

According to Christian, the officer administered the physical test and Christian passed, but the supervisor on duty insisted on a breathalyzer test. He failed with a low number. In California, even if a driver passes all the sobriety tests and is found able to drive, he or she can still be arrested for blowing over a .08 blood alcohol concentration. It makes sense to some degree because the blood alcohol level and its influence on one's ability to drive might still be increasing as the body processes more alcohol; this test is repeated at the scene to show whether the blood alcohol level is increasing or decreasing. At any rate, Christian was arrested and his car was impounded.

At the jail, Christian's blood alcohol level was in the low sevens, so they released him immediately without charging him with anything. The Department of Motor Vehicles suspended his driver's license, however, and Christian was fired from his job. He spent five months looking for another job and landed a few interviews, but he couldn't pass the background check with a DUI (Driving Under the Influence), even though he had not been charged with the offense. This might sound strange, but it is the law in California where driving is considered a privilege as opposed to a right.

Christian told me once that in his ten years of driving in South County, he had been pulled over and had his car searched more than twenty times. He once asked a friend to check his police records and found that he had more than thirty contacts. The police tend to learn who to watch and which cars to search. Most of Christian's searches had occurred while he was using drugs. Probably, the police strongly suspected he was using but just couldn't catch him.

Angie and I had bought Christian a new Nissan pickup while he was in college. Within four years, the interior was torn up and we were constantly working on the wiring under the dash because the police were regularly messing it up as they searched for drugs. I don't blame them for searching the vehicle of a known drug user if they have a legal right to do so. The majority of Christian's friends had been arrested for drugs, and many of them had served time in jail or prison. And since the police knew this, they likely assumed that if Christian was hanging out with known drugs users, he was probably using drugs, too. I would have made this assumption myself.

One day, Christian and I were sitting in the garage, brainstorming how he might be able to get a job while he was banned from driving. We talked about him joining the Air Force and the Navy since he was approaching the age when he could no longer be considered eligible for military service. Christian had tested for the Air Force and scored high. He could have had nearly any job he wanted, except that the Air Force wouldn't commit him to a specific career. So he tested for the Navy and was offered an undersea welder job. While this was a great position and he was excited about it, he had one problem: he was taking Suboxone, which had been prescribed to help him withdraw from heroin, and he needed to stop taking it before reporting for basic training. It is my understanding that he should have been on the medication for only a short time, because according to some, it is even more addictive than heroin. Chris was on it for at least five years.

He started to shave the pills, and eventually, he was just taking dust each day before he quit taking it completely. Angie and I were counting each day as he went through the withdrawals. The first three days seemed to be pretty easy, probably because some of the drug was still in his system. On the fourth day, however, he started to get sick. He couldn't sleep and he was shaking, saying that he felt like he was running. By the sixth day, he was vomiting, experiencing diarrhea, and was unable to do his community service work at a local church. The seventh day was a little better, but the eighth and ninth days were unbearable.

On the afternoon of the ninth day, Angie called and asked me if I wanted to go to Taco Tuesday. I said, "Yes, I will leave work at four." When I got home, Christian was pretty sick and didn't want to go with us. This was unusual for him because he loved to eat out with us. I would always tease him and say, "Christian is always up for a free meal out with Mom and Dad." He always smiled when I made such comments. That day, however, he asked Angie to bring home a couple of tacos and said if he felt better, he would eat them later.

When we arrived home after dinner, Christian was vomiting over the toilet and hemorrhaging from his nose. He said he felt extremely ill. Once again, he was shaking and he felt like his feet were running. The life of a drug addict is not a good one. For Christian, as long as he had been on Suboxone he had seemed to live a pretty normal life. But he had a dream of being a successful deep-sea diver and welder, which meant getting off the drug. Eventually, that evening, he felt a little better and had a good time playing with his two-year-old nephew, Noah. When Noah shot Christian with a single-shot toy gun, Christian went to his room, came out with a semi-automatic toy gun that held dozens of darts, and shot Noah fifteen to thirty times. The two laughed and hugged, and Noah said, "I yuv you, Uncle." Noah wasn't old enough to be able to say "Christian," so he just called him "Uncle." They had a good time that evening.

My pain as I write this is nearly unbearable, but I want readers to understand that getting off drugs can be as dangerous as continuing to take them.

Christian was also on muscle relaxers for a severed rib from being hit by a motorcycle, of all things, as well as an antianxiety drug. He went to the garage, his hangout, to watch television and try to relax for a while. My last words to him were, "Go to bed, Chris, and sleep it off." I was concerned about him, but I wasn't worried. I regret that I didn't spend more time with him that evening. I'd started a new job the previous day and had to be at work by 6:00 a.m., so I went to bed around 9:30 p.m. I told him good-night, but I didn't hug him. Christian nearly always ended every phone call or "good night" with, "I love you, Pops," and he did that night too. I told him I loved him and headed upstairs.

Read the Label and Do What It Says!

Christian went to the garage with a thirty-two-ounce bottle of wine. It may not have been a full bottle when he took it out of the fridge, but by the next morning, three-fourths of the bottle was empty. The labels on all the meds he took cautioned against using alcohol, but Christian ignored them. He had a problem with alcohol as well, and I'd told him many times that year that he had become an alcoholic. I am not a doctor, but when someone has to drink a bottle and a half every night, in my mind, that's a problem.

I took Noah upstairs to bed with me and left Angie on the couch where she had fallen asleep. I thought I would give her a break from the baby, as he didn't sleep very well.

2:11 a.m., June 18, 2014

Like clockwork, Noah woke up in the middle of the night and cried for his bottle. I calmed him down and told him I would go downstairs to get it for him. As I walked down, I noticed that the television was on and the volume was turned up unusually high, but Angie was still asleep. I picked up the remote and turned the television off. As I headed for the refrigerator to get Noah's bottle, I noticed light coming through the crack under the door that led into the garage. I opened it to see if Chris was okay. He was lying on the floor by my workbench where he always sat. My view was blocked by Angie's car. I yelled, "Christian! Get up and go to bed!" I figured he was asleep since I'd found him right there, passed out, a few months earlier. That time, I had just covered him with a blanket. This time, I yelled for Angie to wake him, as I had to get back to Noah. I grabbed a baby bottle from the fridge and headed up the stairs.

2:12 a.m., June 18, 2014

My life changed forever for the worse, as did the lives of my wife, my remaining son, my daughter, Christian's aunts and uncles, and his friends.

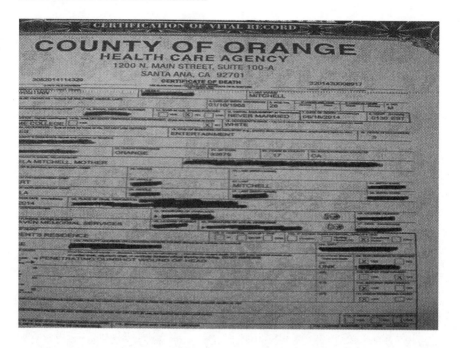

I heard a loud scream. It was Angie. "Oh no! Bob, there's blood and a gun!" I turned and ran back down the stairs and into the garage and saw what Angie saw: my best friend, my son, lying in a four-foot diameter pool of blood with his eyes closed, as if he were peacefully asleep. I could see a bullet hole behind his left ear with a trail of drying blood running to the floor. Angie had picked up the gun off the garage floor and placed it on the workbench. To this day, I don't remember seeing the gun, but I must have because I knew it was Christian's .40 caliber handgun. I checked his pulse. He didn't have one. He was cold. His body was on the floor, but his head was elevated, lying on top of the wheel of a moving cart.

I saw the wound so clearly. I soon wished I hadn't, because for the next month, I could not get that sight out of my head. It was in front of my eyes all day, every day. I spoke with a psychologist about it and she said it was a sign of serious trauma.

I grabbed Angie and the two of us virtually crawled back into the house, wailing. I hugged Angie as we both screamed and cried uncontrollably. For the next few moments, I forgot that Noah was sitting in my bed directly above us, waiting for me to bring his bottle upstairs. Those five minutes or so must have been absolutely terrifying for the little two-year-old boy who had already lost his mama and hadn't seen his dada for three months.

I got Angie to the couch and dialed 911. The operator couldn't understand me as I told her, "My son is dead. He shot himself in the head and I need some help here. I don't know what to do!" I must have hung up the phone because the operator called back and asked how old Christian was, what he looked like, what I looked like, and, of course, where the gun was. Even though I answered all her questions, she called back several more times. I must have kept hanging up. Finally I thought of Noah, went upstairs, and brought him to Angie. She tended to him, which probably helped her achieve some level of self-control. Noah, on the other hand, was hysterical because he had been listening to all our screaming and crying below him.

I went to the garage to be with my son, but I knew I couldn't let Angie or Noah see him. Angie had already seen too much. So I stood just inside the garage door, watching over my son while I waited for a deputy to arrive. Probably ten minutes later, an officer walked up my driveway alone. As he approached, I pointed to where Christian's lifeless body was lying. I couldn't speak at the time. I went back into the house and was hugging Angie when another officer arrived. I asked the officer if he would call our pastor, Brett Peterson, and ask him to come over. Pastor Brett is a Chaplain with the Orange County Fire Authority and a Professional Services Responder with the Orange County Sheriff's Department, so I guess I thought the deputy knew him. I found Pastor Brett's phone number and the officer called him for me.

While we were waiting for Brett, I called Bobby and told him to come over. I told him what had happened over the phone and he sounded just like Angie and I had after we had first seen Christian. I had never cried like that before, but when I heard Bobby's response, I immediately thought back to Cheddar Bob and that horrible phone call from Bobby that day in Simi Valley.

Pastor Brett arrived quickly. He knows Angie and me very well, as well as all the issues our family has endured, but this surprised him as much as it did us. We had had no idea that Christian was suicidal.

I also called Angie's brother, Steve, and pleaded with him to come to the house. Angie's brothers live a hundred miles north of us, so they couldn't get here for a while, but I knew we needed all the family we could have around us. Steve called his and Angie's brothers, and they all jumped in their cars and were at our house in a few hours.

The police department also sends out volunteers to be with people in situations like this. Two of these volunteers, both of them women, came over and spent the next two hours with us and Pastor Brett.

I spent a lot of the next hour with Christian as we awaited the arrival of the coroner. I couldn't get close to him because the police had declared his body a crime scene, but I felt I was with him as long as I was in the garage where his body lay. The officers guarding the scene asked me several times if I would feel better inside the house, but I needed this time with my son. I fell to the ground a few times and the deputies came over and spoke with me, but they did not touch or hug me. When a father experiences a loss like this—this father, anyway—he needs everyone to hug him. I felt that way for the next three weeks.

The scene was horrendous, for lack of a better term, and I have thought about it nearly every waking moment since. But because Christian had a bullet entry wound and no exit wound, I knew we could have an open casket funeral service, which I knew Angie would want.

People usually want to know if their friend or loved one suffered any pain as they were dying. From what I know about Christian's knowledge of ballistics, and what I know of the ammunition he used, he didn't feel any pain from the moment he squeezed the trigger. He used an extremely lethal hollow-point bullet that expanded and fragmented the moment it was fired, which is why there was no exit wound. His heart had obviously continued to pump since he lost so much blood, but he had not struggled and his eyes were closed. If only he had asked for help. Angie and I are used to helping our children. Perhaps that is why he never asked.

Although Christian ended the pain that he was feeling, Angie and I, Bobby, and Hannah will feel the excruciating pain of that gunshot wound each and every day we continue to live. Christian knew what Angie and I had been through with him and both his siblings, and I know he didn't want to cause us any more pain. People who commit suicide are not thinking rationally. I know that Christian never thought about the pain he was about to cause all of us for the remainder of our lives—more pain than anyone can imagine unless they too have suffered the suicide of their child.

Finally, the coroner arrived. I was surprised to see him dressed like a member of the bomb squad. He was wearing full-body armor from the neck down. After I thought about it, though, I realized that coroners have to walk right into murder scenes and probably don't often know where the murderer is. At any rate, when he arrived, the officers asked me to go into the house and not come out until after the coroner came to see me and left with Christian's body. I have a degree in law enforcement, and therefore, I had studied this process in my coursework, so I knew what he was about to do with my son's remains. I did not want to be there to watch.

I went into the den and spent the next two hours with Angie, Pastor Brett, and Bobby. With the flash of a muzzle, this family joined the thousands of Americans who suffer the tragic loss of a child each year. We are not alone. In just one minute, I can think of Coach Tony Dungy, Pastor Rick Warren, Coach Andy Reid, one of my former bosses, and countless celebrities who have outlived their sons in one way or another. I now understand their pain.

There were five or six deputies at the house until the coroner left. Looking back, I do wonder why there were so many deputies there, but they were all comforting. I asked if any of them knew Christian and they all said no. This was comforting to me, because as far as I knew, he hadn't been involved with the police (other than his DUI) for at least four years.

The Coroner Prepares to Leave

At about 5:30 a.m., the coroner came in and handed me a plastic bag containing Christian's personal effects. He tossed Christian's cell phone onto the coffee table in an angry manner and said, "When you can, take a look at the text messages on the phone. It was lying on ground next to his hand!"

"What is on the phone?" I asked him.

"I can't tell you now," he said. "Just look at it when you can. This is why he did it!"

He offered his condolences, gave me his business card, and told me how to clean up the mess in the garage with bleach and water. We said good-bye and each officer shook our hands, offered their condolences, and left. Some of the deputies appeared shaken up, as well. I think it hurt them to see people so broken as Bobby, Angie, and I were. I truly was a broken man at this point, and I pretty much remained so for months. Never in my life had I felt so empty and worthless. I had been just upstairs while my son had been suffering so much from depression that he'd thought this was the only way to end his pain.

5:45 a.m., June 18, 2014—Now What?

The pain was over for Christian, but for me, it wasn't just another event in our lives caused by one of my children as usual. I had no idea how to cope with it! There is no turning back from death. Christian was gone forever.

Bobby went to the store and bought some bleach. I mixed it with hot water and proceeded to clean the garage floor where Christian had bled out. Pastor Brett offered to do the clean-up, but I felt this was the job of a father, and I remember saying something like that to him as I whimpered while cleaning. Bobby was throwing up, so I told him to get out of the garage and not to come in until I'd finished cleaning. Pastor Brett stayed and prayed over me for the forty-five minutes it took to clean up.

Afterward, I went back into the house and spent some time with Angie and Bobby, and we began to plan our day. My stomach hurt terribly and continued to hurt for the next month. It felt like I had swallowed a handful of rocks.

While we waited for Angie's brothers to arrive, I went back out in the garage by myself, fell to the ground where Christian had died, and bawled my eyes out, begging God to "Take me." I went to the driveway and looked for my neighbor Al hoping he would come out and hug me. I remember how badly I needed to be held. I stood in the driveway, looking up to the moonlit sky, and screamed at God, "Why Christian? Why not me, Lord? Please, God, I cannot take this pain. Please kill me now so I can be with You and my son!"

I heard a voice in my head say, "I know, I know, I know your pain!" I am certain it came from God. *Of course He knows,* I thought to myself, as I regained some self-control. He gave His Son so that I, Christian, and all mankind can leave our earthly bodies one day and be with Him for eternity. He felt the pain I was enduring as only a parent who has lost a child could.

Then Bobby wrapped me in his arms and held me tightly as I wailed. I begged him to be sure that was the last terrible event I would ever have to live through with my kids. Later, I begged the same of Hannah. Both she and Bobby promised Angie and me that, for the rest of their days on earth, they would do all they could to spare us any more pain. Honestly, I would rather be dead than continue this life without my son, but I will live on because I know that God has a plan for me and He is not finished with me yet. When He is, He will take me to be with Him and my son. I think I speak for most parents when I say that, if I could, I would give my life to have Christian walking this earth again.

Angie's brothers and cousins arrived around 6:00 a.m. I'd planned to go to work at 7:00 a.m. and tell my new boss that I was going to be out for a few days. I had only been with the company for two days, and I had been hired to lead it out of a major compliance mess with the U.S. Food and Drug Administration. We had just fourteen days to develop and submit a complex plan to the agency, and I was already going to miss work!

Angie's brother Gabby insisted on driving me to work. He dropped me off and waited for my call to pick me up. In the meantime, I informed my new bosses, met with my employees, and gave them some action items for the next five days. My bosses were more than understanding. In fact, they were shocked that I had even come in to talk to them, just five hours after discovering Christian's body. To me, it just wasn't something I could do over the telephone. Although I had only been with the company for two days, everyone treated me like family. They hugged me and told me they would be praying for us.

After Gabby returned to take me home, Angie, her brothers, and I headed off to look for a cemetery and a mortuary for Christian's funeral service. Meanwhile, Pastor Brett left to contact the Orange County Jail chaplains to plan how we could inform Hannah of the loss of her brother and best friend. I had serious concerns that if the deputies didn't already know what we were telling Hannah and they saw her come unglued, she might end up chicken-winged. You will read about this experience later in Hannah's chapters.

By noon, Angie and I had quickly looked at three mortuaries and two cemeteries and learned the processes we needed to sort through. Pastor Brett had the arrangements with the jail all set and we planned to meet at 1:00 p.m. to inform Hannah of Christian's suicide. Angie and I, along with Pastor Brett and Pastor Lisa (Hannah's jail chaplain, whom she had grown close to), would break the news to Hannah. Lisa had become an awesome mentor for Hannah, who, at this time in her life, planned to leave the jail in October and attend Bible College.

1:00 p.m., June 18, 2014

We met Pastors Brett and Lisa outside the jail and planned how to break the news. Now, understand that one can only "meet" with a prisoner by talking to her on a telephone while looking at her through a thick glass window.

Lisa would start by letting her know what had happened. As we walked around the corner, we saw Hannah sitting at the phone, waiting for a surprise visitor. She appeared a little shocked when she saw the four of us, and I learned later that she had initially thought she might be getting out early. Lisa sat down, picked up the phone, and told Hannah that Christian had passed away. Like the rest of us, Hannah was overwhelmed with immediate grief. But my little girl is a very strong woman. Perhaps she gets her strength from her mother.

After Lisa spoke with her, Angie and I and Pastor Brett took turns talking and praying with her. Lisa was absolutely amazing! She has the calling of our Lord and it shines through her. I thank God that He placed Lisa in Hannah's life.

Also, while Hannah was incarcerated, four good friends from our church visited her nearly every Saturday. Tim and Sara Phaler and Layne and Sarah Edwards ministered to her, read books with her, and prayed with her. For an inmate, the isolation is torture. This outpouring of love from our friends (who had not known Hannah before she went to jail) kept Hannah studying God's Word, praying, and staying hopeful for her future. I believe their interaction with Hannah was God-ordained and that it played a key role in helping her to receive this news and put her faith in Jesus as she headed back upstairs to her bunkies.

Before we left the jail, Pastor Brett asked Hannah, with such wisdom, "How can I pray for you specifically?"

Hannah's response was, "Please pray for and look out for my mom and dad." This was a real sign of maturity in Hannah. She wasn't asking for anything for herself. She was legitimately concerned for Angie and me. When substance abusers are using, all they care about is when and where they can get their next fix. Now Hannah's concern was for us. This was a key sign of transition to a new normal!

When we had finished visiting with Hannah, Angie prayed with her over the phone as we placed our hands on Hannah's through the glass. As Angie was praying, the inside of my head became like a movie theater. I was watching a scene unfold. I saw a beam of light coming down from the sky and Christian walking toward it, followed by Hannah, who was holding Noah's hand and walking out of the Orange County Jail. As Angie finished praying, my vision faded away.

As difficult as it was, we needed to leave and Hannah had to get back to the women's tank, where she was housed with forty other women.

We left the jail, went back to the mortuary we had chosen, and signed the paperwork to have Christian's body moved there so the caretaker could prepare it for the funeral. We bought a new suit and shirt for him, and I planned to give him one of my favorite ties to wear into eternity.

Finally, we left the mortuary and headed home. On the way, we called the cemetery and made an appointment for nine the next morning to choose a burial spot and make the final arrangements.

When we arrived home, we discovered a lot of family members waiting there, and we needed every one of them. Angie and I both struggled with various fears and felt empty when other people weren't with us. I had never cried so much in my life. I felt like my insides were literally being ripped out of me.

Despite the pain, however, survivors have a lot to do immediately after a sudden death. Angie's cousin Julia selected photos for the funeral, and her cousin Marisa catered the food for the meal at our house after the funeral. Their support and involvement was a huge blessing.

At noon on the day of Christian's death, my employer sent us a huge fruit basket. Sheri, the head of human resources, and Rachel, the operations manager, delivered dinner that evening, spent some time with us, and prayed with us. What a loving bunch of coworkers and supervisors God placed in my life, just in time for me to go through my most painful experience. God is so good! He knew in advance what was going to happen and He prepared a place for people to care for me, even at work.

The Cell Phone Text Messages

When I read through the text messages and looked at the embedded pictures on Christian's phone, I knew why the coroner hadn't wanted to talk about it, especially in front of Angie.

I learned that at about eight thirty the evening before his death, Christian had been drinking wine and suffering from Suboxone withdrawal when a friend started sending him text messages. His pain and suffering from the withdrawal combined with the wine and the text discussion had all been more than he could handle.

Christian and his friend had texted each other for nearly two hours. Christian sent his last text at 11:30 p.m., which read, "I am killing myself," along with a picture of him loading his gun with two hollow-point bullets. There was no reply to his last message.

According to the coroner, Christian had died at approximately 1:30 a.m. on June 18, 2014. I don't understand the two-hour gap in time, but since there is so much I will never understand about this senseless loss, the gap issue is trivial.

I read the text messages, and although they helped me to understand more of what he had been thinking and why he was so distraught, there was much I still didn't understand. But then, this is suicide. I am not sure anyone can ever completely understand what a suicidal person was thinking at the time of their death.

September 2, 2014

On September 2, 2014, at approximately 11:00 a.m., I started receiving text messages from the friend of Christian who had been texting with him the night of his death. We wrote each other, and the evening of June 17 started to come together for me. I won't say it made sense, as suicide will likely never make sense to me, but I did begin to get some clarity.

At 11:00 p.m. that same day, I accepted a phone call from a blocked phone number. Normally, I don't accept blocked numbers, but I did answer this one since I had gone to bed but the phone wouldn't stop ringing. It was Christian's friend. We spoke for an hour, and a lot of questions were answered for me as well as for Christian's friend. I had assumed Christian was on the phone when he pulled the trigger because it was lying next to him, but I didn't know for certain until this conversation confirmed it. It became clearer to me as we talked, that Christian had been very distressed, but able to hide it from Angie and me, for the most part.

One thing I am sure of is that this event changed my life—along with Bobby's, Hannah's and Angie's—forever. We still suffer the pain of this loss nearly every moment of every day. We all cry nearly every day and have to work at not appearing to be sad—all because of a loved one's drug abuse.

Christian made some really bad decisions in the adult years of life. Many of these bad decisions had to do with his choice of friends. Although he was clean for six years, many of his friends were either active drug addicts or recovering drug addicts.

Approximately 9:00 a.m., June 18, 2014

Angie and I went to the cemetery and selected Christian's grave site as well as ours so that when our time comes to leave this earth, we will be buried next to Christian. Julia stayed with us for a few days, and Angie's brothers and Marisa returned for the weekend. We needed every minute spent with every one of them.

To this day, it amazes me that Hannah was so strong that she could endure all this pain by herself while she was in jail. I cannot imagine how difficult this was for her. Had she not been right with Jesus Christ, she may have ended up another casualty, but she immersed herself in church, prayer, and Bible study, and I believe our Lord carried her through.

Christian's funeral was scheduled for one week after his death, and Hannah insisted on trying to get out of jail to attend the funeral. The courts normally deny these requests, however, assuming the inmate can even get his or her attorney to file the request. The viewing was set for June 24, from 5:00 p.m. to 8:00 p.m.

At 1:00 p.m. on June 24, I received a phone call from Hannah's attorney. She said, "Mr. Mitchell, get down here now, court room X5. The Judge is going to consider our plea for a compassionate release." I shaved so quickly that I cut myself, and I had already taken my aspirin for the day. I was still bleeding as I drove the forty minutes to the courthouse.

I met and waited with Hannah's attorney until the judge called her to his bench for a consultation. I must have looked pretty strange sitting in the back of the courtroom, holding toilet paper to my chin. The judge spoke with the attorney, and then said to the courtroom and to Hannah, "I said years ago that I would never do this again. I let five people out on compassionate release and none of them came back." He looked at me and said, "I am looking at Hannah's father out there, and he looks like a man who will bring his daughter back." Then he said to Hannah's attorney, "If I let her out and she is not back in this courtroom at 8:30 a.m. on June 26, 2014, will you surrender your license to practice law?"

Hannah's attorney ran back to me and said, "Mr. Mitchell, did you hear that? He wants me to surrender my license if she doesn't come back." She asked me what she should do. In the three months I'd known her, this was the first time I'd ever seen her indecisive. I told her, "I only know what you tell me, and that is that they don't come back. I can't tell you what you should do, but given what you've told me, I wouldn't do it."

She turned away, saying, "I'm going to do it." Hannah's attorney was court-appointed. We were not paying for her service—not Hannah, nor her mom, nor me. And yet, Hannah's attorney told the judge, "I will give you my license if she doesn't come back, your honor." Upon hearing that, the judge issued the order for Hannah's immediate release to attend her brother's funeral.

It wasn't until we were halfway through this hearing that I realized we were asking the judge to release Hannah, completely unescorted, without a deputy or an ankle transponder. So when he released Hannah to my custody, I assured him I would not let her out of my sight and that in two days, we would be outside his courtroom by 7:00 a.m.

Knowing that "immediate release" really means release just before midnight, Hannah's attorney and I walked out of the courtroom and planned for me to return after I had attended Christian's viewing. In spite of all the evil Hannah's judge and attorney saw every day, they were able to see a promise in Hannah's bloodshot eyes, and I am indebted to them for having been compassionate.

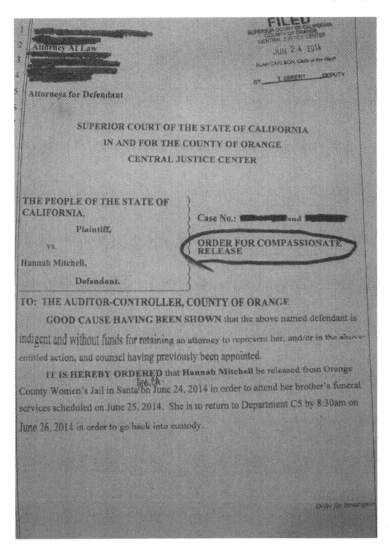

The Viewing

Many came to pay their respects that evening. It meant a lot to me to be there for my deceased son. If I had been allowed, I would have stood guard over his body the night before the funeral.

After the viewing, Julia and I drove to the courthouse to wait for Hannah to emerge from the top of the stairs. We were at the jail by 8:45 p.m. for another long wait. What we saw for the next three hours was quite sad. Dozens of inmates were released, one at a time, none of whom looked like they would be out for very long before they returned to jail. Most, if not all of them, appeared to have lived through a long and difficult past with drug abuse or other forms of substance abuse. Most of the inmates released that night had no family or friends to pick them up. So they stood outside and cried, as they had nowhere to go.

11:45 p.m., June 24, 2014

Finally, my baby girl emerged from the top of the stairs, carrying a bag full of her personal belongings. We hugged as she went through the metal detector and all the way to the car. We talked about the funeral plans during our forty-minute drive to the house, and Hannah shared her plans for her part of the funeral. She had prepared the first sermon of her life, and it was quite long. I was wondering how we would do so much in just an hour-long funeral service.

Back at the house, Hannah was greeted by Noah, Angie, Bobby, and other family members. We all cried and prayed together and finally went to bed around 3:00 a.m. We had gotten used to not sleeping over the past week, but we needed to try to get some rest before the funeral. Angie slept with Hannah in our bed, and I slept on the floor by the bedroom door so Hannah couldn't get out without stepping over me and, hopefully, waking me up. The next morning, we ate breakfast and left for the funeral, which was to start at 11:00 a.m.

Wednesday 11:00 a.m., June 25, 2014

The funeral was a beautiful tribute to an awesome young man. Pastor Brett and Pastor Chris spoke first, and then I spoke, followed by Hannah, and finally, my good friend Bron Draganov, who delivered some comforting words of hope as he described the grieving process and some choices that we'd be making. Five years earlier, Bron had lost his son, who was a good friend of Christian's, also to suicide. Hannah's reading was closer to a sermon; it was God-inspired and truly honored her brother. At one point in the service, I read a brief letter from Bobby to his deceased brother. Bobby was too torn up to speak or read.

Toward the end, I dismissed the kids to go outside with my sister-in-law, and then I addressed the drug addicts in the chapel. I begged them to get help and to let this be the last of several friends to die from drug abuse. I then turned the remainder of the service over to Pastor Brett, who led an altar call. Nearly twenty people committed their lives to Jesus Christ at Christian's funeral.

Next, we loaded up the hearse and drove to the cemetery for the graveside burial, where Pastor Brett spoke once again and we buried our son, brother, uncle, cousin, best friend. Angie is European, and many European cultures stay until the grass is replaced. So we did it the European way. Family members and friends picked up flowers and tossed them into the grave, and then we asked the cemetery workers to replace the dirt as we looked on.

We proceeded back to the house for some food and fellowship with friends and family. At some point that night, we finally went to bed to get some much-needed sleep. Hannah and Noah were inseparable for Hannah's entire thirty-hour release, and the two of them had a great time. I slept on the floor by the door once again to be sure Hannah didn't try to escape.

June 26, 2014

We were up and heading to the jail the next morning. Once we knew we were within a few minutes of the courthouse, we stopped for breakfast at McDonalds. This would be Hannah's last good meal for the next three months. After breakfast, we drove around the corner to the courthouse, went through the metal detector and up the stairs to room X-5, and arrived an hour early.

We waited for the room to open, but 8:30 a.m. passed and the door still hadn't opened. It remained locked until 8:49 a.m., which meant we were technically in contempt of court. This may sound ridiculous, but this is our legal system. It is entirely possible, although not probable, for one to be found in contempt of court for not being able to penetrate a locked door in order to fulfill a commitment to the judge.

We were the first people in the courtroom, and we walked straight up to the bailiff. He remembered us. He checked Hannah in and dismissed us to go have coffee while the courtroom prepared for the day. After we had had a cup of coffee, we returned to the courtroom to wait for Hannah's name to be called. First up, however, were several small cases that had to be discussed briefly. The room was packed so full that people were standing in the back and Hannah and I couldn't even see the judge.

"Hannah Angelia Mitchell," the bailiff at the front of the room called.

"I am here!" Hannah yelled as we stood up, but the judge didn't hear her. He called her name in an irritated tone, and Hannah emerged from behind the crowd in the back. The bailiff spoke to Hannah first, and then the judge said, "Thank you, Miss Mitchell. Thank you." The judge then turned to the courtroom and said in a deep, loud voice, "Let it be documented and known in this courtroom that this young woman is a person of high integrity." He repeated this statement as Hannah was handcuffed and taken back to her cell.

As I turned to leave the courtroom, the judge called my name and thanked me twice. Crying and wiping my tears, I thanked the judge with a broken voice.

Drug abuse buried my twenty-six-year-old son, my best friend, with whom I had done everything. I am lost without him, and others have told me that I will probably think about that sight on June 18, 2014, every day. Indeed, I remember my loss only seconds after I awake each morning. However, I stand firm on the Scriptures and my faith in my Lord.

In Genesis 37:35, when Jacob is told the lie that his son, Joseph, is dead, the Bible says, "And all his sons and all his daughters arose to comfort him; but he refused to be comforted. And he said, 'For I shall go down into the grave to my son in mourning,' thus his father wept for him." Though only a short time has passed since Christian's death, I agree with Jacob; I will mourn Christian's death until I take my last breath. How sad it is that drugs were the root cause of many of the bad decisions in Christian's life, culminating in the permanent damage that he inflicted on so many of us and that we will suffer until our heavenly Father takes us to be with Him. I lean on the following Scripture each day:

> For I am persuaded that neither death nor life, nor angels nor principalities nor powers, nor things present nor things to come, nor height nor depth, nor any other created thing, shall be able to separate us from the love of God which is in Christ Jesus our Lord.
>
> —Romans 8:38–39 NKJV

I will see my son in heaven where he is no longer suffering from drug addiction, alcohol abuse, or the loss of his girlfriend. But it is not God's will that any of us should take our own lives. Even though the Bible is clear on this, God is merciful, and I believe He does not judge a person who does not have a sound mind. Christian committed his life to Christ at a Harvest Crusade at Anaheim Stadium many years ago and was baptized at Saddle Back Church shortly after his rebirth. I am comforted in knowing that he was saved.

Lessons Learned

Never take for granted a day that you get to spend with your loved ones. Only God knows how many opportunities remain. Tell them you love them, hold them, kiss them, and know how short life is.

Don't hold grudges! Christian was my best friend to his death.

All drug addicts are liars. I must repeat this once again. Do not believe their lies and don't fall for their manipulation of your love for them.

Intervene as early as possible. Spy on your loved ones if you even suspect they are using or abusing.

Even when you catch abusers in the act, they will likely try to convince you that you're not seeing what you know you're seeing. The night of Christian's death, he assured me he was heading upstairs to bed to sleep off his withdrawal. He wasn't.

Some doctors are licensed dealers of mind-controlling prescription drugs. If your loved one is buying directly from the doctor, find out why! Study the drugs the doctor is selling and look closely at their side effects and interactions with other drugs.

Depression is not always apparent. Watch closely if you have any concerns for your loved one.

Don't let your loved one mix meds and alcohol.

Choose your friends carefully and cut your losses early. If your son or daughter is hanging out with the wrong crowd, *do whatever it takes to end those relationships.*

Never allow an addicted individual to withdraw without being under the care of a reputable licensed professional. The risks of suicide are far too high to take the chance of not receiving this guidance and care.

Of the more than 40,000 Americans who commit suicide each year, 75 percent of them are male, and substance abuse is a common risk factor. The signs of pending suicide are not always obvious, so keep it at the front of your mind as you deal with an abuser. Suicide is always possible, whether the signs are there or not.

Chapter 7

ONCE BUSTED

"I called on the Lord in distress; The Lord answered
me and set me in a broad place. The Lord is on my
side; I will not fear. What can man do to me? The
Lord is for me among those who help me; Therefore I
shall see my desire on those who hate me. It is better
to trust in the Lord Than to put confidence in man."

—Psalm 118:5–8 NKJV

If you are reading this book and experimenting with drugs, or abusing any
substance that can get you in trouble, I encourage you to check out the
legal issues you are playing with in addition to the possibility of becoming
addicted and even being killed by your substance of choice.

Most states have what they call "special circumstances." Get to know
the law if you are planning to violate it, or you may be as unpleasantly
surprised as Hannah was when she was arrested and booked for *six* felony
counts with *two* strikes.

The first thing an inmate is asked in an arraignment (where he or she
appears in court in a cage, handcuffed and shackled) is whether he or she
is willing to waive his or her constitutional right to a speedy trial. Since
I am not an attorney, I am not qualified to give professional legal advice,
but in my opinion, waiving this right hurt Hannah's case. Unfortunately,
I couldn't afford a good attorney who would spend an enormous amount

of time preparing Hannah's defense, and I received virtually no time from our court-appointed attorney.

The courtroom is a busy place whenever the judge is not present. Both the court-appointed defense attorneys and the prosecutors were always unprepared for Hannah's case, along with the dozens of other cases I sat through. They hurriedly scrambled through files in the back of the courtroom because they knew the judge would be coming out in just a few minutes. Occasionally, one of the attorneys would toss out a guilty plea offer without any preparation.

Prior to Hannah's arrest on the six felonies, she was offered thirty days in jail—five times over a period of ten months—for a hit-and-run that was never proven to have happened. The prosecution eventually dropped this, but it took Hannah five trips to the courtroom where she had to sit for seven hours at a time just to get five minutes of negotiation between the unprepared defense attorney and the unprepared prosecutor.

If Hannah had not waived her right to a speedy trial, the attorneys would have had to prepare and present their evidence within either thirty or sixty days, depending on the circumstances. Instead, each time Hannah appeared, either the deputy DA or a public defender requested a continuance for another couple of months. At least one time, Hannah's attorney wasn't even present. She had called a friend to take her place and request another continuance.

Even though the judges get angry when neither side is ready for a hearing, they seem to tolerate it. The judges don't see what occurs in their courtrooms when they step out, but they must know since they were once in the same positions. What they do see is somewhat-prepared, professionally presented requests for a continuance.

In their first meeting, Hannah's attorney told her she was guilty of every charge and she just needed to "get over it!" Initially, she wanted Hannah to plead guilty as charged and take three to five years in prison. In the end, Hannah's attorney worked out what the judge referred to as "a very good deal." Considering the starting point, I think Angie and I agree. I am not sure how Hannah feels about it, but she knows it saved her life. It's all about negotiation, and the accused parties and their families need to be patient with the process.

Guilty Until Proven Otherwise

In the jail system, there is no difference between the accused and the convicted. For the safety of the officers who work in the jail, everyone is presumed to be guilty until proven otherwise. This may sound like a violation of the civil rights of the accused, but it is not. They accused are only presumed innocent until proven guilty in the court system; this does not apply to the incarcerated.

Once in the jail system, the inmates must follow the rules, join the gang of their race, act like a racist in order to survive, and keep their distance from other races. They must never surprise a guard and must always be prepared for daily verbal abuse and sarcasm from the officers. Inmates where my daughter was jailed were allowed out of their cells for two hours each day. During this time, if they had "money on the books" they could call friends and family on the phone while the officers listened to their conversations. The cost for using the telephone is astronomical. A ten-inch by eight-inch pillow cost Hannah $8.10. I joked with her about how cheap she was. When she returned to the jail, she refused to buy another one and instead, used her clothes for a pillow for the next three months.

To Bail or Not to Bail?

You will need to decide if you are going to post bail for yourself or your loved one. If you do and you or your loved one are found guilty, you will then have to check in and serve your time. By the time Hannah got through at least four continuances and was finally offered an acceptable plea bargain, she had already served half of her sentence.

Hannah accepted a guilty plea to three counts, from six felonies to one with a strike and two misdemeanors. The seventh count, misdemeanor hit-and-run, was dismissed. Hannah still says the witnesses concocted all but one charge.

If you are going to play with fire, expect what is called "over-filing." I am told by defense attorneys that prosecutors often file many charges that they anticipate tossing out in plea negotiations. In Hannah's case, they over-filed probably six of the seven charges, and she was probably guilty of only one. If you are addicted to drugs, you would be lucky to end up with the deal Hannah was offered—if you don't end up dead, period! If you are a loved one—again, do everything you can to intervene. Angie and I had threatened drug dealers many times to the point that they refused to sell drugs to Bobby or Christian.

If you are using drugs, know the laws because they escalate quite quickly, and it can be an eye-opener when they read the charges to you.

One day, while I was awaiting Hannah's court appearance, I saw an individual slapped with "possession of concentrated cannabis." He turned white as a ghost in disbelief. The word *concentrated* changed his future. Rather than paying a small fine, he was off to northern California for a thirteen-year stay in a state prison. I mentioned this to a career pot-smoker at the fitness center, and he was shocked. He is a user of concentrated cannabis but had no idea what the penalty is when convicted for possession of it in relatively small quantities.

Because Hannah hadn't stopped fighting back after she'd won the fight, she received a felony strike for assault after her attacker had been subdued. This charge comes with serious jail time, and after that, without the mercy of our Lord, she'd never have been able to get a job with that showing up in any background check.

In California, if Hannah had stopped fighting back when she saw her opponent's bloody nose, she would have been charged with only a misdemeanor. Since she took another shot at breaking his nose after he was subdued, it escalated to a violent felony. In California, this is normally known as a "wobbler," meaning it could be a misdemeanor or a felony, but Hannah was honest and admitted to the police, whom she had gotten to know over the years, and trusted, that she had done what some of them had told her to do on several occasions—but of course, they hadn't really meant it.

If you choose to bail either yourself or your loved one out of jail, if you pay for a bail bond, you don't get back that eight to ten percent you or your loved one will pay out. In most states, you needn't bother seeking a bail bondsman; they will be calling you continually, unless you are the one in jail, because it is normally a felony for a bail bondsman to call an inmate.

The Penalty Phase

After the arrest and conviction comes the penalty phase. Don't count on avoiding jail time just because of overcrowding!

Once either you or your loved one is out of jail and on "formal probation," then, depending on how busy they are, the local police could be breathing down your neck. One time, when I met with our local police chief after the shooting of an unarmed young man in our neighborhood, he said, "Mr. Mitchell, I don't want my cops sitting behind the hardware store killing time; I want them stopping people on probation and searching them and their cars."

In August, I spoke with Ryan, a young man at my fitness center whom I've gotten to know. Ryan had shared a story with me about his brother, who was soon to be released from prison after a long stay. I stopped going to the club for two months after Christian's death, but one day after I returned, I ran into Ryan and asked how his brother was doing. He said, "He was kicked out of rehab." I told him I was sorry to hear that. I hadn't realized his brother was even out of prison because I hadn't seen him for two months. Ryan told me his brother had been out for two weeks when his parole officer checked his medicine cabinet and found over-the-counter cough medicine. He said, "My brother was immediately kicked out of rehab, which then puts him in violation of his parole agreement."

If you are a drug abuser, I hope this causes you to think twice before continuing to abuse drugs. If you are the parent of an abuser or suspected abuser, or even if you're not, you must require your eighth-grader or high-schooler to read this book, discuss it with you, and summarize each chapter before he or she gets his or her first driving permit. Once your son or daughter is busted, life changes dramatically. It is nearly impossible to comply with all the requirements the states impose on probies. In the chapter titled, "Once Busted," Hannah covers her life in jail. Her story is not for lightweights!

Lessons Learned

Law is complicated. Even the attorneys don't know everything. Hannah's attorney didn't even know she would not be allowed to have a driver's license in California for five to forty-five years if she pled guilty.

In California, the Department of Motor Vehicles can suspend a license without the courts and without a trial.

Learn what your punishment is going to be before you get busted or before your loved one pleads guilty. Once you're busted, life will never be the same for you or for anyone close to you.

Be prepared for bureaucracy if you or your loved one are breaking the law!

Save your money. Everything has a fee and it is always unreasonable.

Chapter 8

ONCE CONVICTED

By Hannah Mitchell

"Tribulation and anguish, on every soul of man
who does evil, of the Jew first and also of the
Greek; but glory, honor, and peace to everyone
who works what is good, to the Jew first and also
to the Greek. For there is no partiality with God.
For as many as have sinned without the law will
also perish without the law, and as many as have
sinned in the law will be judged by the law."

—Romans 2:9–13 NKJV

It was the morning of March 30, 2014. What I thought was going to be a joyous day of celebration in seeing my brother Bobby and his fiancé get married ended with cops, tow trucks, breathalyzer tests, drug tests, blood tests, and handcuffs. Instead of being in family photos at the wedding, I was photographed by a CSI photographer, courtesy of the Orange County Sheriff's Department. Busted again—and this time it would be the first and hopefully last time I would be sentenced. It was around 11:00 a.m., the beginning of a long stay at the Orange County Women's Jail facility. The sun was shining and the air was crisp, not too hot and not too cold—the best weather a bride could hope for on her wedding day.

I woke up in the morning for the first time that entire week! I was a meth addict, and since I generally didn't sleep, often there was never any sleep to wake up from. But the night before had been the first night that week that I had actually gone to sleep. I would have stayed up that night as well, except there was one problem: I was out of dope (crystal meth). Meth users and addicts, like abusers of other drugs, often hurt when they withdraw, which can and often does lead to arguments that quickly spin out of control and turn into fights. I was feeling pretty ill, and the meth that my drug partner had used the night before had been purchased by me, with my money.

I was mad. My partner used up all my dope! I got into a violent argument with him that morning. This is a normal part of life for drug addicts. I don't know if taking an excessive amount of prescription antidepressants will actually kill one, but at that moment I didn't care and I hoped it would. I swallowed approximately fourteen pills. The pills didn't kill me, but they certainly didn't help the situation. The arguing continued and then progressed to fighting.

Then, I suddenly realized that I had just one hour left to get to the wedding, I jumped in my car and tried to leave the scene. Of course, I was in no condition to drive, being in a state of hysteria and having been beaten up. As I tried to back up, the fighting started again. This time from inside the car as my assailant dove through the back left window. Inadvertently I shifted into drive and my car and I ended up crashed on top of a retaining wall, waiting for the police to arrive.

My phone was dead and no one was going to let me call my mom or my dad. All the witnesses would be against me. I had no one to defend me and I knew this was going to mean a trip to jail, but I had no idea how much the district attorney would throw at me. When the police arrived, they were shocked. A female officer who knows me from other calls to the house, checked me out and said, "Goodness, Hannah, what have you done to yourself?" I looked horrible and my face was chronically broken out with meth sores. She went on to say, "Hannah, you used to be a beautiful woman!"

Once again, a life of drug and alcohol abuse was going to ruin another precious day for me. Instead of attending my brother's wedding, I headed to jail, wondering what was going to happen to Noah. After hours of interviews and the cops mapping out the scene of the crime, I was taken to Orange County Women's Central Jail and booked on six felony counts with two strikes. In California, anyone with three strikes will spend the remainder of their life in prison. I was one strike away from never again being a free person.

In thirty minutes, I was at my new home in the receiving center, which is infamously known in the criminal world as "the loop." The loop is where inmates get processed. It is a long, slow walk that ends several times at different check-in stations. For some reason, the loop is always cold—in the low sixties. I had to remove any body piercings, my tattoos were recorded, and I was fingerprinted and photographed. I was then interviewed to see if I was a 51/50 (a threat to myself or others).

After the interview, I was booked on "attempted murder, corporal abuse, elder abuse, child abuse, and driving under the influence of alcohol and/or drugs while attempting to cause great bodily injury." My bail was set at $600,000. I was in shock! I had never intended to injure anyone. The "victims" alleged that I had been trying to use the car to kill or injure several people. I had no one with me to back up my position, so I was defeated from the outset. To this day, I cannot understand how the prosecutor could file all of those other charges. DUI I could understand.

After the officer informed me of my charges and the bail amount, he asked more questions, such as how I felt about the charges and whether it depressed me. The officer was trying to determine whether I was a danger to myself. "Of course it depresses me," I said. "What do you think?" So then the officer determined I was a suicide risk, which triggered another process of being routed to a mental health professional for more interviews. At the end of the interviews I was informed that I was going to spend twenty-four hours in the medical wing. I had already heard about this experience from others, so I begged the mental health professional not to put me there, arguing that I was okay—but it was too late.

Next, I was routed back to another holding cell, where I joined two other women, one with no teeth who had just been arrested for purchasing four grams of meth. The other told me that eight months earlier, she had been using meth and not watching her young daughter, who walked out of the house and was hit by a car and killed. I felt bad for her and thought of how that could be Noah if I didn't get clean. As I spoke with this woman, it was clear that she had no idea what day or time it was, a sign of meth use commonly referred to as "being on tweaker time."

We were asked to stand up and follow a red line to the next room. A door opened and we followed the line to another door that opened as we approached. We were now in the area referred to as "property." In this area, the deputies record every item the bookie is wearing—jewelry, clothes, money, purse, shoes, panties, everything the bookie had with her when she was arrested, right down to the color and size. This is when the bookie becomes an inmate. The inmate is issued jail clothes and moved on down the loop.

We moved along and arrived at what is called a holding cell. The three of us were freezing and tired, so we all lay down on concrete benches. The other girls fell asleep, but I stayed awake.

In addition to being surrounded by killers, in jail you are surrounded by illnesses! For six months, I was exposed to people with HIV, hepatitis, herpes, syphilis, chlamydia, staph, and countless open, bleeding, weeping wounds.

Finally, the door opened and I knew we were about to be "housed" (taken to our cells). I knew this from experience, as I had been arrested the year before for hit-and-run with my third car in four years. In five years, I crashed four cars.

As the deputy led me down a long hallway, we walked by the door I was expecting to enter to get to the cells. But when we didn't enter that door, I started to wonder where we were going. This was a long walk and a part of the loop I hadn't seen before. Finally, we entered a room and a nurse came and greeted the officer. The officer turned and walked back in the direction we had just come from as the nurse told me to follow her. She led me down a short, dimly lit hallway and we ended up at door number nine. It had a solid iron door with only a slot for food to be slid through to the inmate. The nurse opened the door and told me to enter and remove all my clothes except for my "granny panties" and to put the clothes back through the slot. I did as she told me and another nurse came and slid a bright-orange plastic dress through the slot for me to wear. In the tanks, this orange dress is referred to as the "party dress."

What I didn't know until later is that I was being housed in the infirmary on suicide watch. I spent the next seventy-two hours there. I was not allowed any phone calls and could see nothing but the inside of my protective cell. Inmates in these cells don't have pillows, blankets, cups, eating utensils, or anything else they could hurt themselves with. I slept well the first night, or day—I am not sure which it was. I was awakened by a nurse who slid some food through the slot to me, without any utensils. Inmates in these cells eat with their fingers.

On my second day, or night, I heard the strange and horrible singing of some church song coming from another cell. I looked through my little window to see whatever I could. There was a girl across from me peering through her slot. She saw me and stopped singing to ask my name. "Hannah," I replied.

"I am Christine," she said. "Do you believe in Jesus?" she asked.

I hesitated for a second, not because I didn't believe, but because no one had asked me that question for as long as I could remember. Finally, I replied, "Yes, I do believe in Jesus."

She said in her soft voice, "Well, God bless you, Hannah."

I was bewildered, thinking to myself, *Here I am in a looney bin, wearing a plastic orange dress and talking to a girl who is singing songs about Jesus. Have I really hit bottom? And why is this Christine at peace in here?* I walked over to my bed, lay down, and started crying, thinking about Noah and my brother's wedding, wondering why I was in there. "My parents will get me out soon," I kept telling myself. I didn't realize my parents had no idea where I was—other than in jail—or why I wasn't calling them, as I had during my prior visits to the jail.

Over the course of these seventy-two hours, all I could do was sleep, think about my uncertain future, try to eat whatever the guards slid through the slot, and take the meds they provided me. Toward the end of the second day, I heard Christine yell out, "Hannah, are you okay?" I told her I was scared and didn't know why I was in there. She explained that I was there so I would be cleared of any threat of injury to myself. "Just try to sleep and see if they can get you a Bible to read," she said. I told her I would and lay back down.

After three days in the infirmary, I was finally deemed not a risk to myself or others and was moved to what is called a "tank." A tank is a jail cell that houses several inmates in one room. My tank housed forty women in an area approximately twenty-five feet long by fifteen feet wide, so it was quite crowded. It included four sinks, two showers, and four community toilets right where everyone could see you doing your business.

Once in the tank, I quickly made friends. The first woman to greet me went by the nickname Lucky. She was only twenty-one years old, but was already serving her third drug-related sentence. *Not very lucky*, I thought to myself. Lucky introduced me to my fellow inmates. The first thing I noticed was how much better off I was than the others. Very few of them had any family, and they all looked like they had rough lives. Most of the inmates I was with didn't have any teeth.

As I looked around at all the other girls, I thought to myself, *I'm a pretty girl, but these ladies would never know it because they're seeing me with huge sores all over my face.* Out of all my tank mates, I stood out the most at this point in time, and I was quickly labeled "Tweaker"! *Is this the way I want my son to think of me when he gets older?* I thought.

When I was finally allowed phone calls, I called my parents, who told me what was happening with my case as I broke down, crying. Until I made that call, I really didn't understand how much trouble I was in and how severe my charges were. My court date was set for two weeks after my arrest.

I was afraid to cry in front of the girls because I didn't want to show weakness in front of them, so I did my best to cry in secret as I settled in. Jail life can be dangerous, and there is a clear pecking order and even seniority among the inmates. Showing weakness can set up inmates for a difficult stay. Some of the women I was with were pretty hardcore, experienced at crime and experienced at doing the time. You can be in jail for only a DUI and yet be the bunkie of a murderer. Separation of inmates is primarily based on their behavior while incarcerated, not the crimes they committed on the street. Surprisingly, I received a lot of support from my fellow tank mates and ended up forming positive and lasting relationships with some of them.

My First "Toss"

In my third week, all of us in Tank 5 were going about our business when five cops barged in, telling us not to move, to stop whatever we were doing, and to file into the day room. I asked my bunkie what was happening and she said, "It's a normal procedure called a toss." A toss is when the cops raid the inmates' cells or tanks, go through everyone's bunks and belongings, and toss them around the room. The goal is twofold: 1) to search for contraband and 2) to show the inmates who's in charge. There are only a few things that cannot be on an inmate's bunk—learning which things usually comes with experience. Banned items include chow (jail-provided food), newspapers, extra jail-issued clothing, and anything that has been altered in any way from its intended use. I had a stack of comics from the newspaper stuffed under my mattress, jail-made black eyeliner (makeup made from colored pencil lead, toothpaste, coffee, and water), and two altered razors (razors with the bottoms broken off, leaving the blades unguarded)—I used one to sharpen my pencils and the other to cut fellow inmates' hair, which they wanted me to do once they found out I was a cosmetologist. The intruders found it all!

When the toss was over, they told us to leave the day room and "Clean up your tank!" The tank was a disaster. Everyone's personal belongings had been thrown around like a tornado had hit the room! Family photos were all over the floor with stuff spilled on them and mattresses and pillows were tossed about. I had to wade through stuff to get to my bunk, and when I finally reached it, I found it trashed. Nevertheless, I cleaned it all up and then went back to looking at magazines and drawing in my coloring book.

Later that night, after lights out, my bunkies awakened me to tell me my name and bunk number were being called over the speaker and I needed to get into full jail issue. As I was waking from a dead sleep, it took me a minute to process what they were saying. Then I heard an angry voice over the loudspeaker: "Mitchell, H-5-10, wake up, get up, and come to the gate in full jail issue." In regard to knowing the time, being in jail is like being in a casino. There are no clocks. I rarely had any idea what time it was, but I estimated that it was around 11:00 p.m. I threw on my jail issue, hurried to the gate, and waited for it to open. "Hurry up and wait" is another theme of jail life. I noticed three others in my tank were doing the same drill, so I was relieved it wasn't just me. The gate opened and we walked to the door while a deputy unlocked the second iron door. He said, "Keep your hands in your pockets and walk straight out to the red line, turn, and face the wall." Next, another deputy directed us, "Go downstairs to the guard tower and wait to be called by your name." One by one, we were called to a window and told what the deputies had found in our bunks during the toss. I was the last inmate to be called, after all those before had been excused to go back to their housing locations. When I was called to the window, the deputy recited what had been found on my bunk and informed me that I was receiving my first write-up. My violations required that I do five hours of extra duty washing the walls of the medical wing, and I was required to begin right then.

Another deputy called for an inmate worker to get a bucket of water and two sponges and bring them to me. The deputy then pointed to the wing I was to clean and told me to scrub the walls. The section I had to clean was where the high-profile inmates were held if they were determined to be dangerous to themselves or to others. I started cleaning the walls and noticed something rust-colored running down them. I didn't think anything of it until I saw the color of the water change to the color of blood. That's when I realized, *I'm in the medical wing, cleaning blood off the walls, and without gloves.* After about twenty minutes, I mustered the courage to ask a deputy if I could get a pair of gloves. He didn't like the idea, but reluctantly and sarcastically got me a pair. I continued to clean for about two more hours as I headed down the hallway toward an area known as "the hole." The hole is where inmates who have gotten into serious trouble in jail and the completely crazy or dangerous people are held.

As I worked my way down the hall, I saw a girl awake in one of the cells. Even though she was locked behind the door, I was scared stiff and noticed several signs on the doors warning of a very dangerous occupant. I hurried to clean the wall so she wouldn't see me. As I scrubbed the floor, I looked up and suddenly discovered this girl staring directly into my eyes. I jumped back and stared at her. She continued to stare back, so I just waved. She smiled and waved back.

I picked up my bucket and moved down the line. After about three-and-a-half hours, I'd finished cleaning the medical wing and I had serious plans to never be found in violation of anything ever again. I was also convinced that I would do my time without enjoying the "privileges" of being an inmate worker. Thinking the deputy would give me a break since I'd already finished cleaning that area, I moved toward the guard tower, hoping the guard might say, "All right, you're done." Apparently, however, I wasn't finished. So I headed to the infirmary and started cleaning some more. This was where I had first been housed for observation and forced to wear the orange party dress.

As I began cleaning, I heard a girl talking to herself. Again, I was scared and a little freaked out, so I quickly worked my way along the hallway.

To protect the deputies, the jail is designed as a series of block-wall hallways with cells along the walls. The deputies are rarely in these hallways. Instead, they watch most inmate activity on cameras, except for the activity that occurs in the camera's blind spots. Realizing the cell Christine had been in was off camera, I moved over to see if she was still being held there. I saw little red-headed Christine sleeping and my heart broke for her. I finished cleaning and headed back to the guard tower. Finally, a deputy asked me, "Are you done?" "Yes, sir, I believe so," I replied. He directed me to leave the sponges in the bucket and go back upstairs to my tank.

I went back upstairs and followed the red line to my tank, faced the wall, and waited about thirty minutes for a deputy to unlock the iron door to my cell. Tired from being up all night, my arms sore, I got in bed still wearing my jail issue. The moment I lay down, the speaker came on instructing us to get up for count and chow. It was 4:30 a.m. I am certain that they made me wait outside my tank until just a few minutes before wake-up just to have fun with me.

There is a lot of discipline shelled out in jail. For some inmates, jail is the first time they have had to follow basic rules. Jail is not for the faint of heart, however, and it comes with its own set of rules. Before Christian's death, I had actually become the senior inmate in my tank of forty. This entitled me to several perks, but the one I enjoyed the most was that I got to be the first one to read the daily newspaper. After I returned from Christian's funeral, however, I was housed in a two-person cell for the remainder of my time and was allowed to spend only two hours each day in the day room. Previously, in the tank, I could spend most of the day in the day room. The two-person cell didn't even have enough room for its two inmates to walk past each other, and I had to learn to bunk close to pretty serious criminals.

After my violations, I thought the officers had a more aggressive attitude toward me. They often singled me out as though they were looking for opportunities to be verbally abusive to me.

Child Protective Services (CPS) negotiated a Wednesday for me to visit with my mom and Noah. Wednesdays were not normal visiting days, but since my son was so young, these special visits were mandated by the courts. On Wednesdays, the cops let us visit longer than normal hours for the sake of our kids, not for the sake of the parents. Like all other visits, these were "no contact," which meant we spoke on the phone, through glass. Nevertheless, Noah and I had an awesome time. I had finally arrived at the point of not crying and pitying myself, but truly enjoying my son. When the visit was over, I was happy and excited to return to my tank and share with my bunkies what a pleasant time I'd had with Noah. But God had a different plan, another lesson in humility for me.

As I was climbing the stairs, I saw some cops at the top of the stairs in the middle of the hallway. I did what I was supposed to do. I stopped on the stairs and turned to face the wall until I was told to do otherwise. After about five minutes, I was told to "go back," meaning to go to my cell. Then it dawned on me that I'd forgotten to put my hall pass in the pass box. When I turned suddenly to reach behind me to do so, a deputy walking up behind me just happened to be next to the box at that moment. She screamed at me for getting too close to her. I apologized and realized I'd startled her.

Suddenly, from behind me, another deputy threw me face first into a wooden door, grabbed my arm, and bent it awkwardly behind my back and over my head while she pulled my hair with her other hand. Later I had serious bruises all over both arms. The inmates call this process "being chicken-winged," and it happens to most inmates at some time during their sentence. The deputies then lectured me like a drill sergeant. "Why are you trying to jump my partner?" one officer asked.

After a few minutes of verbal abuse, I was then "escorted" (dragged) to a bench and told to "take some time out." For the next four hours, I sat facing a wall in handcuffs. If the Lord's plan was to humble me, He certainly did! What had started out as the best day I'd had in a month ended with a serious lesson in humility and respect for authority.

I matured in jail. Some don't. Some just keep coming back. I got right with my Lord and I am not turning back.

During my stay, I missed my brother's wedding, my son's birthday, Easter with my family, Mother's Day with my son and my mom, Father's Day with my dad, my mother's birthday, and the fourth of July, though we could hear the fireworks from somewhere nearby. I missed spring and summer and, most of all, I missed being a mother to my son for six months.

If you are a drug addict or a substance abuser, don't let it get this far. *Stop now*. Get help!

Lessons Learned

Once busted and convicted, it is no longer just about you! Jail is a consequence for wrongdoings that result from the bad decisions we make, and it hurts a lot of people.

More punishments follow once you become a number and put on the blue jumpsuit. If you get to go to the roof, you will see daylight for two hours each week, and you will be depressed as you look out, see freedom, feel the sun, smell the tamales being cooked at the jail entrance, and hear the sounds of people who are more responsible than you were!

Jail is not the end of the road. You'll have a harder time if you don't learn to survive and comply. You can grow and mature in jail if you choose to.

God was able to get my attention in jail. I heard His voice and learned to love Him and myself. Thanks so much to Pastor Lisa Cram.

Chapter 9

MITCHELL, ROLL IT UP!

"And when Herod was about to bring him out, that
night Peter was sleeping, bound with two chains
between two soldiers; and the guards before the door
were keeping the prison. Now behold, an angel of the
Lord stood by him, and a light shone in the prison; and
he struck Peter on the side and raised him up, saying,
"Arise quickly!" And his chains fell off his hands."

—Acts 12:6–7 NKJV

My perception might be different from Hannah's, but I believe that doing the jail time is the easy part. If you or your loved one is currently incarcerated on a felony, you might be in for a shock at the branding that comes with the conviction.

One month before Hannah's release, we started looking for a place for her to live. Because she had a child, she could not be with him for more than six hours each week until she was living on her own, employed, attending all the classes and probation meetings the state had assigned her, passing random drug tests, and more. It didn't take us long to learn that *this* is really the hard part, much more difficult to comply with than sitting in jail with coloring books, coffee, and newspapers.

We learned first that apartment complexes don't normally rent to felons. That meant we needed to find a room for her to rent. Next, we discovered that individuals seeking a roommate don't want a roommate who's just left jail. To solve this problem, and to be sure Hannah was moving into what I called a "sterile apartment," I rented a one-bedroom apartment near our house. I planned to sleep on the couch a few nights each week so I was in compliance with my lease agreement while Hannah slept in her bedroom. We would be bunkies.

At approximately 11:00 p.m. on September 28, 2014, in the jail, Hannah received the page, "Hannah Mitchell, roll it up." This is the initiation of the inmate release process. At 2:30 a.m. on September 29, 2014, Hannah was released from the Orange County Jail.

This picture was taken the moment Hannah appeared, free but for the shackles of the Orange County Sheriff's Office. The sign behind her is strikingly appropriate.

Angie and I, Noah, and Sara Edwards, a precious friend from church, were there to greet Hannah and to take her to her new apartment. The girls posed for a few pictures, and we departed as quickly as we could, with hope and faith in our Lord and Savior that our experience with jail was finally complete.

Reunited but not yet reunified! This is Hannah and Noah in the jail lobby, where tremendous pain can be seen in the faces of the inmates' friends and family (the victims) any hour of the day or night.

Angie is on the Left, Hannah and Noah are in the center, and Sarah is on the right. Photo permission granted by Sarah Edwards and Angela Mitchell.

We had to be back in Santa Ana (thirty miles north of our home) by 9:00 a.m. the next morning for Hannah to meet with her probation officer. Knowing how difficult it was to comply with all the rules, I wanted to be with her so I could take notes. We found the office with, of course, no place to park. But even though we had to park a half mile away, we were on time. Although Angie had been told that I could sit in with Hannah, as I attempted to enter, an Orange County deputy told me, "Turn around and leave." So I sat outside on a filthy sidewalk for two hours, watching prostitutes walk past the officers.

There were no chairs to sit on, and women with purses had to find a place to hide them outside the entryway, hoping their purse and its contents would still be there when they finished visiting. While I was waiting for Hannah, I spoke with five others who were waiting for their loved ones to complete their visits, and all of these loved ones had been convicted of and served time for drug-related crimes.

Hannah's probation visit went well. She then enjoyed her first day of freedom. She attempted to arrange the classes she had to attend, but all she got were voice mail messages. We had already been warned that no one would return a call. She just had to keep calling, hoping someone would eventually answer the phone.

That first evening, Hannah came to our house for dinner. At about 8:15 p.m., we were leaving the house to take her to the apartment when a sheriff's car drove by with his spotlight right in my face. Since we live in a quiet gated community where we rarely saw cars on patrol, I assumed the officer was looking for Hannah. And since he quickly turned the light off the moment it shone on me, my assumption appeared to be correct. I sent an e-mail to our local sheriff's captain (the equivalent of a chief of police for a small city in Orange County) to explain what had happened and to ask if he would instruct his officers to keep their lights off our neighbors' houses. He quickly wrote back and said the incident had likely been just a coincidence, not checking up on Hannah. Since this sounded crazy to me, I also checked with a friend at another police department, who also told me it was likely a coincidence. This is the life of an ex-convict on probation or parole, however. Once convicted, all freedoms are up for grabs, including the right to privacy for anyone who encounters the convict. The pain of events past continues for both the ex-convict and the loved ones.

Trick or Treat!

As I write this section, the grandsons are all getting excited about Halloween, which is a few weeks away, so the heading seems fitting. The first time Hannah's probation officer visited her, she told Hannah that she was unlike most of her other probies because she seemed sincere and had a good family to help her get back on her feet. I will never know if Hannah's probation officer was being tricky or honest. "I could drug test you today, but let's plan on it during your next visit in three weeks," she said to Hannah. The next morning, Hannah called in to check her color code (a random process for drug-testing a probie). Hannah's color was called, so she had eight hours to go to the clinic and "pee for them with a witness."

Thus far, Hannah has complied with everything she is required to do, and her probation officer has treated her very well! Don't let a noncompliant offender lie to you about the way they are treated. Check out their stories if you need to. Hannah is pleased with the way she has been treated.

The abuser, as well as his or her friends and family, learns fairly quickly that the police are fighting a war against drugs on the streets, and the abuser's loved ones will be part of the collateral damage. I encourage you to keep your faith. As difficult as it is at times, trust the police as much as you can. It will be difficult because they can be and likely will be harsh with you. At times, you too will feel you are being treated like a criminal. I've had that experience too many times to count.

Hannah's First Few Months Out of Jail

When Hannah was released from jail, no one mentioned what medications she had been on in jail, and no one gave her any advice or recommendations to see a doctor. Hannah was so excited to be leaving that she didn't even think to ask which meds she had been taking.

She was released on Monday morning and, as I previously mentioned, she spent her first couple of days of freedom trying to schedule her classes and adjust to not being taken care of twenty-four hours a day. By Thursday, Angie and I were scared to death that Hannah had lapsed into a severe depression. She never mentioned suicide, but you can imagine what Angie, Bobby, and I were thinking: *No, this cannot happen again.* I tried unsuccessfully to get her to see the doctor and get on some meds. By Friday morning, Hannah was so depressed that she couldn't even walk. All she could do was cry and plead to go back to jail. Later, we learned this desire is quite common in newly released inmates. Some of it stems from the security of being in jail, while the rest comes from the uncertainty of the future, as the former inmate now has a multitude of things to accomplish. To add to the depression, anxiety, and fear, we learned that many inmates are tranquilized with anti-anxiety meds and antidepressants. They must not simply stop taking these meds cold turkey, because the withdrawals cause more anxiety and depression than they were experiencing before they began taking the meds. Consequently, they have to withdraw under a doctor's care. I am still shocked that an inmate can be released in such a manner. Once Hannah saw her doctor, who placed her on medications to deal with her new stresses, as well as the withdrawals, she was back to her positive self in just a few days. Later, she was able to get off all the meds.

Adjusting to life as a free women, Hannah attends a parenting class three times a week, a batterers class once a week, a drug and alcohol class one night a week, and random drug testing at least once, but as often as four times a week. All of these classes are mandatory, and they cost a lot of money. Many, if not most, former inmates cannot afford the classes or the transportation to get to the classes, and they end up back in jail within a few weeks of being released. Fortunately for Hannah, Angie is her taxi driver, and she and I are loaning her enough money to get through the first year of probation. Hannah keeps track of this part of her sentence, just as if she were still in jail. A sentence is exactly what it is. Just because offenders are released from jail, that doesn't mean they are finished serving their time. Hannah's sentence continues for another fifty-two weeks from the first night she started her classes. After that, she will remain on probation and drug testing for up to four more years. I am glad for this part of the deal. It can take years to recover from the cravings of drug addiction.

When Hannah is not doing her time, she is blessed to assist a professional hair stylist two days a week at one of South Orange County's best hair salons. This was another miracle in Hannah's life. She walked into the salon one day to have her hair lightened and walked out with a job. She had no idea the salon was owned by Christians until she talked with the stylist who was doing her hair. The stylist asked Hannah what she did for a living and Hannah told her about her time in jail, receiving Christ, and that she was a stylist looking for work. The stylist told her the salon had an opening for an assistant. Hannah interviewed after her hair treatment, and she got the position. God is great!

It has been six months since Hannah's release, and she is progressing well. She is enjoying freedom, walking with our Lord, and loving Noah.

With God's grace and mercy, she will live the life our Creator planned for her. The rest of this chapter is being lived out as you read. Please pray for Hannah, Noah, Bobby, Angie, me, and Bobby's boys as we continue to press on and see what else God has in store for the Mitchells of South County.

Lessons Learned

A convict's sentence doesn't end with the call to "roll it up!" The jail time is clearly the easiest part of the conviction. The most difficult part is complying with the mandates that come with the conviction and resisting Satan's pressures to return to a life that will drive the felon to end up in jail again.

The temptation to return to friends of the past can seem overwhelming, but it must be resisted!

Former substance abusers must always see themselves as at risk of returning to the abuse. They must do all they can to shelter themselves and avoid all the tempters.

They must also stay immersed in the Word of God and replace their old friends with good ones!

Don't let a non-compliant offender lie to you about the way they are treated by their probation officers. Check out their stories if you need to. If they are being "mistreated," it is likely because the probation officers have reason to suspect.

Chapter 10

FREE INDEED

"Therefore if the Son makes you free,
you shall be free indeed."

—John 8:36 NKJV

Like a lot of people who find themselves having an apostle Paul experience (being locked away in jail), Hannah began reading a Bible, and she committed her life to the service of Jesus Christ. To my knowledge, Hannah had never actually accepted Jesus as her personal Lord and Savior before this time, and she had never been baptized.

While Hannah was still in the jail's tank with forty other women, she began attending church several days each week. She didn't care which particular church she was attending; she just cared that she was out of the tank to learn about salvation, transformation, and being made new. Initially, she had cared more about being out of the tank than about attending church. That changed soon after she entered the jail.

Hannah had one particular pastor, Lisa, who was able to connect with her in a special, God-ordained way. When Hannah and Lisa started meeting via the glass booth/phone each week, Lisa led Hannah to repent for her sins and confess Jesus as her Lord and Savior. From that moment on, Hannah planned to be baptized as soon as possible after leaving jail. Pastor Lisa; Intern Pastor Tim and his wife, Sara; and Sarah Edwards and her husband, Layne, from church met frequently with Hannah. The two couples alternated on Saturdays to share the Gospel with her.

Even though Hannah was surrounded by evil inside the jail, on the outside, she was wrapped in love by Christians who kept her constantly in their prayers. Those who attended their churches prayed for her as well. What with the four of them praying and mentoring Hannah, Lisa mentoring her twice a week, and Hannah's relentless pursuit of Bible studies, Hannah became a jail evangelist. God used her on many occasions to minister to new bunkies. I remember how hurt my little bunkie preacher was for one woman in particular who had driven into and killed a cyclist while under the influence of illegal drugs. Hannah had met the girl once before they were both in jail. She tried to minister to her, but the girl rejected any talk of God and spoke flippantly about how she and her dad were working on a story to cover her doing a hit-and-run while the young man had lain dying in a ditch.

In jail, the inmates like to receive letters. Jail is a sad, lonely, and abusive place. Angie and I and wrote to Hannah every week and sent her pictures of Noah. Hannah wrote to us every week as well, and we spoke on the phone as often as we could. This is critical to maintaining the hope and self-esteem of the inmate.

Hannah, like all inmates, learned to be very creative with everything she did. Inmates get bored and seek activities to pass the time. Hannah used a colored sanitary pad, soaked in water to make a water-based paint, to paint the borders of her letters. She also created comic strips and drawings and stuck them to her letters. I never asked what she used for glue, but I suspect it was toothpaste.

At the end of her second month, I began noticing how spiritually mature Hannah was becoming. She was truly developing into a wonderful Christian woman with her heart focused on serving her Father and reaching out to others who have walked her trails.

Below is my favorite letter from Hannah while she was incarcerated.

August 21, 2014

Dear Dad,

Well, it's my thirty-day mark today and I am celebrating and dedicating my last thirty days with a good ol' diet, hardcore exercising, and tons of book writing! I am sending over your pages, which need correcting. [She is referring to chapters I wrote and sent to her for review and editing]. Do you really think I have a special gift? Lisa says so too. When I read your letter and when Pastor Lisa and I have talked about it, I get the most amazing feeling throughout my body. Even as I am writing this, reading your words about my gift, I get this sensation up from my back and through my arms and upper body. Tears of joy come into my eyes and my hair stands on end, like a breeze went by me. But there's no wind. It sounds crazy, but it's true.

The other day on the roof [where inmates can get two hours of sun each week], there were four girls out there with me. It was a warm day, no movement in the air, just the sun shining. All the girls were talking about was loading up a needle and sticking it in their veins and getting high when they get out. My bunkie was even participating in the conversation, and I promise, I was over in the corner of the basketball court, right beneath the sun, sleeves and pant legs rolled up, all by myself, coloring in my coloring book (this is jail life, yes … a little kid's coloring book), just listening.

My bunkie got high with a baby in her. I am sitting there thinking that this woman is up in our cell crying because she is in jail and away from her newborn baby, and now she is participating in this druggy conversation? I started crying and my heart hurt for these girls. So, still by myself in the corner, I prayed to God, "Please ... please ... help these girls; help them to realize there is more to life and help them to turn to You and find You. Help them see that drugs are not important in life, but their kids and their families are, and so is knowing You."

I was genuinely sad for them. Right as I said amen, wiping my tears from my eyes, a breeze and a small gust of wind went right by my face. I made sure to take notice, but there was absolutely *no wind, no breeze* after that moment. It was God telling me He had heard my prayer. God is amazing, especially with this Mitchell family. I feel His presence every day, no question. I feel His presence more when I talk about Him. That feeling I told you about— it's like a high, but a high I've never felt from a drug. Euphoria, I guess. All we need is God's love and God is love. I am ready to get out and be sober and fulfill God's purpose.

If we submit our will to God's will, we will see His blessings in our lives every day. This is what Hannah experienced in jail, much like the apostle Paul did. When Hannah wrote this letter to me, she had just thirty days of her sentence left to serve. Hannah's jail experience, although a little rough due to a couple of deputies, was the best thing that could ever have happened to her. In fact, I believe her jail experience saved her life, both physically and spiritually, and she agrees.

Angie and I had always heard that the drug and alcohol scene is worse in jail than on the streets, but now, along with Hannah, we disagree! Hannah did see drugs in jail, but they were not as prevalent as they are on the streets. Although the jail experience eroded Hannah's self-esteem, it also kept her safe, and it's where she found her Lord and Savior, who is rebuilding her self-esteem. That's good enough for me! Time will tell, but I believe Hannah is going to be a fine woman of God.

October 11, 2014, Hannah's Baptism

Sarah Edwards led us in some songs and played the guitar while another friend, Tony, played his drum. We invited special friends and neighbors and planned a lunch to follow the baptism. We planned to celebrate like the father of the prodigal son. My daughter was home, safe and saved!

Tim Phaler, a rock-solid Christian brother whom I love dearly, participated in Hannah's baptism along with Pastor Lisa. It was a beautiful autumn Saturday. Tim laid the foundation by teaching the meaning of baptism, and he did the best job of it I have ever heard. There is no doubt that Tim knows what it means to be set free in Christ, and he loves every minute of it.

Pastor Lisa told us the story of Hannah accepting Jesus Christ as her Lord and Savior. While we knew Hannah had committed her life to His service, we hadn't heard the story before. Hannah had only told us that she wanted to be baptized as soon as possible after leaving jail. She never backed away from this desire, so we planned her baptism for the second Saturday she was free.

The picture above is Tim Phaler speaking directly to Hannah on the meaning of baptism. Photo permission granted by Tim Phaler.

Pastor Lisa then followed with the rundown on Hannah's salvation in jail, her response upon hearing the news of Christian's death, and the signs of her Christian maturity that day.

Lisa knew that Hannah was going to follow through with her commitment to Christ. she escorted Hannah to the pool, where Hannah was baptized at 12:45 p.m. We celebrated that day and I maintained my composure. Then we walked to our cars and drove home to continue the celebration of Hannah's new life in Christ.

I worry about her and pray for her every day, as she has a long road ahead complying with the edicts from the courts and reunifying with Noah, but I know she can do it because she can do all things through Christ, who strengthens her.

Pastor Lisa Cram baptized Hannah in the name of the Father, the Son, and the Holy Spirit. Hannah rose from the water a new creature in Christ, forgiven of any and all sins of her past, and I managed not to cry. It was truly a miraculous day! Photo permission granted by Lisa Cram.

When I started writing this book, I had no intention of writing a faith-based book or a book about God's power, but when God is the center of your life, how could it be any other way?

The Lord has seen my family and me through more crises than most could ever imagine. I haven't even touched on a fourth of what Angie and I have been though, but you have read enough.

The Lord intended this book to glorify Him using the Mitchell family. Let it be so! If you are not yet a committed Christian, recognize His love for you and let Him have His way. Commit your life to His service now.

Lessons Learned

There is peace in knowing that a loving God created you and wants to have a personal relationship with you. Seek Him out, pray, listen, read His written Word, and seek guidance from your pastor(s) and Christian friends.

No one on this planet is promised an easy life. Angie and I can certainly attest to the fact that being born again doesn't mean you get a free ride, but it does guarantee that you will not be alone on your journey. God is with us, and one day, Angie and I will be with Him and Christian in heaven—and now, Hannah will join us too! Rejoice in the good news that He is all around you in the midst of chaos.

Chapter 11

GETTING HELP FOR
THE ABUSER

"No temptation has overtaken you except such as
is common to man; but God is faithful, who will
not allow you to be tempted beyond what you are
able, but with the temptation will also make the
way of escape, that you may be able to bear it."

—1 Corinthians 10:13 NKJV

Bobby reached the conclusion that the first thing he needed to do was to get away from his friends. He moved to Arizona, became drug free, and has lived free of dependence for more than ten years now.

Christian was able to become free of his addiction to heroin by taking prescription Suboxone. You've already read about how that didn't work out, so I won't repeat it.

Hannah was incarcerated for six months, just long enough to feel the effects of freedom from dependence, and she liked the feeling. She told me later that she had forgotten how it felt to be sober, not under the influence of drugs, and not suffering the effects of withdrawal. She says now that she will never use again.

Friends and family members can play a role in motivating a drug addict or an alcoholic to get help. Once the abuser is receiving help, family members can be reinforcers and encouragers, but it is the abuser himself or herself who must decide to get dependence-free and stay free.

If you or a loved one are at this tipping point and want treatment for drug addiction, the National Institute on Drug Abuse offers a guide to help you and your loved one determine which treatment program to choose. The five questions the guide asks are listed below, and the website for the institute is listed in Chapter 13, "Resources."

1. Does the program use treatments backed by scientific evidence?
2. Does the program tailor treatment to the needs of each patient?
3. Does the program adapt treatment as the patient's needs change?
4. Is the duration of treatment sufficient?
5. How do twelve-step or similar recovery programs fit into drug-addiction treatment?

No matter what your circumstances are, I cannot help but believe that, as long as the abuser wants to be helped, he or she can be cured of this horrible disease of addiction and lack of control of his or her own body.

Pray for your loved one and help them to find the help they need.

Chapter 12

SUPPORT GROUPS
FOR VICTIMS OF
SUBSTANCE ADDICTS

In my research I was not able to find a lot of support groups specifically for the victims and loved ones of substance abusers, and most of the ones I did find were local to a community.

I recommend loved ones of substance abusers or addicts do their own local research, find a group that seems to be what they are seeking, reach out to it, and give it a test run. We have a mega church where I live, called Saddleback that has a support group for virtually every need. Most churches can point you to the resources you need to reach out.

Some of the broad-reaching support groups I did find are listed below.

Action Family Foundation (800) 367-8336
http://www.actionfamily.org/content/support-groups

The Foundation (For Family Victims of Substance Abuse)
(401) 305-0718
http://dranitasfoundation.webs.com/

1-800-799-SAFE (7233) National Domestic Violence Hotline 24 Hours A Day 365 Days A Year

Chapter 13

RESOURCES FOR THE ABUSER AND ADDICT

A simple internet search will turn up thousands of resources for addiction and recovery. I have found many of these to be very resourceful. Below I have a listed a few, in addition to one very important lifeline.

National Suicide Prevention Lifeline 1-800-273-8255

Celebrate Recovery at Saddleback Church, Lake Forest, California:
http://www.celebraterecovery.com/

Foundation for a Drug Free World (888) 668-6378
http://www.drugfreeworld.org/about-us/about-the-foundation.html

The National Institute on Drug Abuse (877) 643-2644
http://www.drugabuse.gov/publications/seeking-drug-abuse-treatment-know-what-to-ask/introduction

Alcohol and Drug Rehab Finder (888) 397-6047
http://www.alcoholanddrugsrehab.com/?_vsrefdom=ppc&gclid=CJatreyJmcICFQdsfgod1QcA2A

Partnership for Drug Free Kids (855) DRUGFREE
http://www.drugfree.org/know-child-using/i-know-my-child-is-using/

National Institute on Drug Abuse –
http://www.drugabuse.gov/about-nida/other-resources

SAMHSA (877) 726-4727
http://www.samhsa.gov/

U.S. Department of Health and Human Services –
https://www.childwelfare.gov/systemwide/substance/resources.cfm

Recovery.org (888) 255-1403
http://www.recovery.org/

National Substance Abuse Index (877) 340-0184
http://nationalsubstanceabuseindex.org/

www.bettyfordcenter.org/Addiction-Help
(866) 805-7530

Adwww.interventionservicesinc.com/

The Prelude Foundation (Orange County CA.) 949.608.7370
Email: info@preludefoundation.org
Prelude Foundation
PO Box 3901
Tustin, CA 92781
http://www.preludefoundation.org/about.htm

Chapter 14

CONCLUSION

"The Lord is my shepherd; I shall not want. He makes
me to lie down in green pastures; He leads me beside
the still waters. He restores my soul; He leads me in
the paths of righteousness for His name's sake. Yea,
though I walk through the valley of the shadow of
death, I will fear no evil; for You are with me; Your
rod and Your staff, they comfort me. You prepare a
table before me in the presence of my enemies; You
anoint my head with oil; My cup runs over. Surely
goodness and mercy shall follow me all the days of my
life; and I will dwell in the house of the Lord forever."

—Psalm 23 NKJV

Raising Drug Addicts is not the end of the story for the Mitchell family.
I accept whatever else God allows to be put in my path. I pray for His
strength and guidance every day, and I continue to count the minutes that
go by each morning before I think of the death of my son. Again, I share
Derwin L. Gray's pain and I know what he means by "holding an entire
generation at gunpoint." The drug abuse of my kids has taken its toll on
my family and even on the lives of my grandsons. It is a cruel and tortuous
experience to love a substance abuser. It is only by His grace that Angie
and I have survived to be able to dedicate the rest of our lives to helping
Noah and his cousins. Without Christ in my life, I possibly would have

abandoned my children in their abuse or perhaps even taken the route Christian took on June 18, 2014. Although I have never considered such a drastic measure, I have no idea what I might have done had I not lived a life committed to Christ.

While we rejoice daily in Hannah's progress, the hostage-taking is not over with. Hannah has quite a schedule to complete each week, and random drug testing often interferes with it. Angie has committed her life for these twelve months to being Hannah's chauffeur. We are not complaining, however, because our little girl is walking with our Lord and trying to do the right things right.

All of us are hurt beyond belief over the suicide of our son and brother. People often tell me they cannot imagine the pain of the loss of a child, and I have no words to respond to them other than, "You are right. You cannot imagine!" Feeling this pain every waking moment of our lives has, however, put the loss of our Creator's Son into perspective for us. *Our God* placed *His Son* on this earth to die the most painful death anyone can endure, and *He did it for us!* We often think of the pain Christ suffered, but tend to neglect the pain God suffered when He saw His Son dying on the cross. Putting Christian's death into perspective in this way helps me cope with it while I continue to seek the new normal in my life.

When I started writing this book, Christian was alive and well, and I spoke of normalcy and observing change in the life of a substance abuser. When I wrote about the shifting of *normal*, I had no idea that by the end of this book I would be writing about the new normal in a different way—in my life, as well, as I cope, learn to live without my son, and live with the images I saw in my garage that morning on June 18, 2014.

At the time that I submit this book for publication, it has been nine months since Christian's death. In the first six months, I thought I would never get through this, and yet I am getting through it—we all are, together.

At Christian's funeral, my friend Bron spoke of the new normal we would find if we pursued it. I hear his words in my head quite often, and I am beginning to experience the new normal he talked about. Although it had been very painful to lose my parents, it was different—they had been very ill. Christian had just turned twenty-six; he was less than half my age at the time of his death.

Why Us?

I cannot count how many times I have been asked the question, "Why has this all happened to you and Angie—do you have any idea?" The answer is always the same: "I have no idea why us." What I do know is this: although our trials have tested our faith in Christ, we remain committed in our belief in our sovereign Father. I will share a couple of the things that have occurred to reassure us that He is God and that He has my son with him.

One Friday morning shortly after Christian's death, Angie was on the phone to Hannah while she was in jail. Hannah shared with Angie a dream she'd had the night before (a Thursday). In this dream, Hannah and Christian were river rafting and loving every minute of it. After a while, they were both sitting on the side of the river, watching others as they rafted by. Hannah turned to look over at Christian, who was sitting next to her. He was looking at her through a bed of sunflowers. Hannah and Christian had never been river rafting before, and neither had ever expressed any interest in it. Nonetheless, in this dream, they were enjoying being together as they tested their rafting skills.

Angie was shocked when Hannah told her about this dream. In the appendix, you can read about another dream that Hannah had. She apparently has a gift in this area. Angie told Hannah that she had visited Christian's grave the day before (Thursday) and placed some sunflowers on it. Never before had sunflowers had any association with Christian, Hannah, or Angie. Angie had simply picked them out because she thought they were more masculine than most flowers. Was this a coincidence? I don't think so. I believe it was a message from our Lord.

I mentioned this to Pastor Brett and was surprised at his response. He wasn't at all surprised by the dream. His response was, "That is the way heaven is going to be. It is not surprising that a dream like this would be revealed."

More Evidence

The day we had to go to the jail and break the news to Hannah about Christian's death, she got a new bunkie. Her new bunkie had been arrested the day before, and Hannah's other bunk was empty, so the new bunkie ended up there instead of in one of the hundreds of others.

Hannah had befriended this young woman when she moved in the day before and had already begun to minister salvation to her. When Hannah returned from hearing the news about her brother, her new bunkie cared for her, as did the other women in the tank.

We worried about Hannah, and we knew we would not hear from her for another day or so, as inmates' time is limited. God is bigger than us, though, and He had a plan to comfort us. We learned that night that Hannah was okay and that she was being loved and cared for by the other women in her tank. We learned this through the other young women's parents!

Hannah's new bunkie was bailed out by her parents, and she was sharing with them about this girl named Hannah who had just been told that her brother had committed suicide. Her parents knew instantly that it was Hannah, *whom they had been praying for.*

Hannah had never met her new bunkie before. I don't believe it was just a coincidence that she ended up in Hannah's bunk, in that tank, for just a few hours—the most important hours of Hannah's incarceration.

Angie and I attend church with this young women's parents, and we had a common bond with them as of June 18, 2014. They had also lost a son in nearly exactly the same way as we had, due to Suboxone withdrawals. Was it a coincidence that our Lord would use their daughter (an atheist) to bring this message of peace from the Orange County Jail to Angie, Bobby, and me? No!

Orange County is a county of several million, and the jail houses thousands. An atheist might argue that it was coincidence that this girl was the daughter of friends of ours who had suffered the same loss and just happened to attend a tiny but powerful church some thirty miles south of the jail—but the odds are too small. I also believe our Father is working on the heart of this young women and demonstrating His realness to her.

I don't know why us, and I wish it weren't us, but then again, if God has a plan, then it has to be someone. It is my hope and prayer that reading this book has helped you in your life in some way, whether you are a substance abuser, an addict, or a loved one.

While I've been writing this conclusion, my phone has vibrated with a message from Bobby to let me know that Christian's best friend, also named Chris, is turning himself in to the Orange County Sheriff's Department on two outstanding felony warrants in hopes of being moved to a heroin rehabilitation center.

At Christian's funeral, I pleaded with each of his friends to seek help and to assure me that Christian's death would be the last one. Chris made the right decision today. Rather than continue to feed his thirst for heroin, Chris is going to seek help. It takes courage to choose this path, as the addicts know what they are opting for. It is not easy, but it is their only chance of saving their lives.

If you are an addict or if you just call yourself a user, I pray that you will get help now, before it is too late! Let my family's experiences be your guide to seeking permanent freedom from the pains of addiction. Search the Scriptures, pray, and find peace in knowing that your Creator loves you and wants to see you grow through what you are going through. Seek His guidance and listen to His Spirit as He speaks to you.

Chapter 15

DON'T LET IT END THIS WAY!

Final Lessons Learned

Be Intuitive – When your intuition tells you something about your loved one has changed, do not ignore it or brush it off.

Seek divine guidance through prayer and listening.

Investigate – Do not be weak. Do whatever it takes, within the law, to investigate the causes of the symptoms you are observing. If the suspected one lives in your house, leave no stones unturned. Look in every shirt pocket, every jacket, pants, potential hiding place.

Speak to friends of the suspected one. Be observant of their reaction. Do not let up! You may be saving one or more lives!

Seek divine guidance through prayer and listening.

Interrogate – When the time is right, drill the suspected one. Press hard. Be observant of the suspected ones attitude and responses. Question whether what you are hearing is truth or lies. Think about what you read in the book about fits of anger you have not seen perhaps, before the change. Be cautions and do not get physically hurt.

Pull out the drug test and challenge the suspected one to prove his/her point if they are insisting they are not using drugs.

Seek divine guidance through prayer and listening.

Intervene – I am no expert on intervention but I will say this; the one thing Angie and I did in this area that seemed to work, was our personally addressing every dealer we could find and threatening them when necessary.

Our users were already past age 18. If you are dealing with a minor, intervening is a little more in your control. Figure out what you are going to do and do it. Do not worry about being wrong. I would rather be wrongfully questioning my son than planning his funeral.

Seek divine guidance through prayer and listening.

Seek Support – As I discussed in the book, you cannot be alone in this. Seek support.

Appendix 1

AN INTERVIEW WITH HANNAH MITCHELL

Throughout the book I theorized on what I thought Hannah would say or how she felt about certain things but these were my theories, not Hannah's. We decided to interview Hannah on her six month anniversary out of jail and attempt to hit on all the subjects I theorized her positions of thoughts might be. The questions and answers below are the nuts and bolts of the interview.

Question: Hannah; thinking back to one year ago, including all the issues with court, the jail time that followed, and then freedom, what have you found to be the most difficult of these three phases?

Answer: "The most difficult part of the three phases is the third phase, freedom. Real world is difficult. In the jail world we are driven by structure. We eat at predetermined times, shower, and even sleep when we are told to. I had no real worries or any responsibilities while I was in jail."

Question: What do think was the easiest of the three phases?

Answer: "Adapting to the structure and the rules in jail."

Question: You found the Lord Jesus Christ in jail, can you tell me about that experience?

Answer: "I was having a difficult time dealing with being enclosed twenty-four hours a day with very little free time, so I when I heard the guards call for church over the loud speaker, I jumped at the opportunity to attend every service I could. I felt like Pastor Lisa (the jail Chaplain) was addressing every one of the feelings, emotions, and problems I was experiencing at that present time. I felt like the Lord personally influenced Pastor Lisa to deliver specific messages to me at the very moment I needed to hear what she was saying. She and the Lord got my attention and opened my eyes."

Question: I wrote in the book that I believe the jail time saved your life, what do you think about that?

Answer: "Jail did save my life. If I didn't die from the fighting that was associated with drug abuse that would have eventually killed me, then it would have been the drugs that would end my life. Either way, I am convinced that if I hadn't been arrested this last time, I would be dead now or with the next couple of years."

Question: While you were in jail, you mom came to see you several times each week and I came with her on Sundays. Often Noah was allowed to come and visit with you. What was that like and what is your best memory of seeing Noah in the jail?

Answer: "It was always a great thing to be able to see Noah while I was in jail. He would try to come through the glass that separated us and he would tell me through the phone to come over to his side. Sometimes he would say "mommy, come home" and this part was always hard for me but I always enjoyed every minute of every visit with him. Toward the end of my sentence, I almost refused my visits with him quite a few times. It got harder to see him and I just wanted to be with him so bad. Speaking on the phone with Noah through the glass each week was getting like torture or teasing me."

"My best memory of Noah visiting me in jail was when he first kissed me through the glass. During my time in jail I was never able to see him except through the glass that separated us. The first time he kissed me

114

goodbye through the glass, holding mine and his lips against the glass is my best memory."

Question: What advice can you offer to a loved one of a drug addict or alcoholic?

Answer: Offer support to a certain extent but do not offer them money. If they continue the addict behavior, let them work their way through it on their own.

Question: "What advice can you offer to an addict or alcoholic?"

Answer: I don't have any advice. An addict or alcoholic in my opinion will never stop unless or until they want to. No advice will get through to them. I will say this though; as I look back at my living as a drug addict, I now remember how difficult it is to be a drug addict. It is a lot of work; trying to remember each lie so I could keep up the same charades, covering up for missing family events, etc. Being a drug addict is a full time job. I am free now and I will never turn back to the life I traded for the one I have now, being right with God."

Question: "What have I missed?"

Answer: You haven't missed anything.

Appendix 2

CHRISTIAN'S LIFE STORY AND EULOGY

Bob Mitchell, June 25, 2014

Thank you for coming out to celebrate the life of my awesome son and great friend. Special thanks to my new family at (employers name removed) and my former work family at (former employers name removed). Two days before Christian's death I started a new job with a new employer.

All week the one thing people have continued to say to Angie and me is "Christian was the kindest, most gentle person they ever knew, and they all said, "Boy did he enjoy fireworks." Even at supercross races all he really ever went for was the fireworks and the explosions at the finish of the races.

I want to tell you about my son and friend whom I miss so much, but first, let me say this: Angie and I committed our lives to our Father Jesus Christ on October 25th of 1982, and all this time I thought I knew what it meant. I am here to tell you today that I now know what it meant to God to lose His Son for us. It hurts so badly!

Christian Fitzgerald Mitchell, aka "Kerman" (a nickname Hannah gave him at two years old but it stuck for his life) was born in Thousand Oaks, California, January 16, 1988. He was in a rush. Angie could barely hold him off as we waited for mum to arrive from forty miles away. Kerman spent the first seven years of his life in Simi Valley where we had a small ranch house on a huge lot.

Life was good. Awesome birthday parties, always with a piñata. We built a motocross track in the back yard and got Christian a quad runner for his third birthday. Bobby had a Yamaha PW 50 and I pretended to ride one of their little bicycles. We'd line up at the starting gate and Angie would flag the start. I would run with the bike and win every race. We had so much fun!

With a sixty-acre field behind our house, in the winter, when the grass was green we would build and launch rockets over the fence and into the field. The boys would run all over the field, looking for the downed rockets.

Christian played soccer and he was in Awana, and when not doing either, he would be working with Bobby and me to restore my '67 Camaro and later in life, Bobby's '69 GMC.

In 1995 we moved to Trabuco Canyon. I wanted my boys to live in a place where boys can be boys like Thousand Oaks was when my friend Bob and I were growing up. Kerman and Bobby lived life to its fullest. It was a dream come true. Tire swings in the oak trees, ponds filled with bass all around us. Mountain biking, BMX, and building BMX tracks and jumps were daily experiences. Often, the boys would be playing in a tree house in the natural run-off area where mountain lions would walk under them on their way to the pond. Fishing together was daily life and both of them became expert-level fishermen.

Christian continued to play soccer and he started Cub Scouts when we moved to the canyons. He tried Pop Warner football for a week but came home every night crying because the coach was calling him fat. He just wasn't a tough guy. Christian settled in with Scouting. He loved the outdoors more than anyone I know and Bobby was usually right there with him. I think they must have gotten it from me. Christian, Bobby, and I did Boy Scouts all the way to Eagle Scout for both of them. This is a big achievement!

When we were not camping with Boy Scouts we were camping with dirt bikes, target shooting, and blowing things up (trash in the desert), and as Boy Scouts do, we always brought home more trash than we created. Christian always created his own fireworks and let me tell you, he was an expert.

I wore Bobby and Christian out with backpacking but we sure saw a lot of beautiful back country. When Christian was about ten years old, Angie and some friends took the kids to the beach. Hannah was swept out in a rip tide and Christian tried to save her. He caught her but both of them were drowning when Bobby then saved them both. They were given a county award for putting their lives in danger to save another. This is just the way Christian and Bobby are.

In 2002 I was laid off and accepted an offer at Amgen, back in Thousand Oaks. This turned out to be not such a good experience for Bobby or Kerman, or any of us actually. Christian withdrew and didn't have many friends there. His friends were here. In 2004 we moved back to Trabuco Canyon and I promised never to do that to my kids again. Christian finished high school and started attending Saddleback College in pursuit of a business degree.

He had a lot of hobbies but really only four favorites. One was military history. In the military history hobby, one thing he did was trace the war history of my uncle Bill and my dad whom Christian never knew. While Christian was tracing the history of my dad about eight years ago, he stumbled into something. A colonel wrote and told him he had something he wanted to present him, but he needed a copy of Grandpa's death certificate and my birth certificate. Christian sent it all in, and a couple of months later he was presented with a Bronze Star that was awarded to his grandpa in 1962 by President John F. Kennedy; they just could not find my dad to give it to him. So Christian was given the Bronze Star my dad never knew he had earned. I am sure Christian told him all about it last week.

Christian always lived with us and we loved almost every minute of it. He was the nicest person one could meet. We spent hundreds of hours together loading ammunition, testing it, restoring dirt bikes, and yes, we enjoyed seeing the pride he had upon seeing the bikes we had built, bought, and placed in a museum. These bikes will live on and serve as a tribute to Christian. Christian and I completed a nine-year-long project of restoring our house a few months ago.

Christian loved to fish. He'd fish with anyone, but most of the time he was with Bobby. In 2002 Chris and I spent eight days on our own lake in Alaska with my good friend, Bron, and his boys. We had the time of our lives. We caught about three thousand trout. In about 1999, Christian caught, and I believe still holds, the Mission Viejo Lake record for a 3lb 2oz sun fish. It is on the table in the back.

In 2011 Christian and I got this wild idea to race the Lake Elsinore Grand Prix together. This GP is world famous and has gone on for more than forty years. We had a blast. This was so much fun and Christian was so thrilled that he finished. Finishing this race is quite an achievement. He is wearing his finisher pin today and into eternity.

Kerman was content in life. He demanded nothing from anyone and expected nothing. At Christmas, the cheapest and most insignificant gift would mean as much to him as a Mercedes. He just wanted friends in his life, and he had many. He was always being called to help someone in some way. He had a special, humble smile when he was complimented. He always looked like my dad when he smiled. Later in life, Christian and Angie became chef buddies. Christian loved to cook with his mom. I believe he found peace in it and, just like working on the bikes was a special time with me, cooking was a special time with his mom. Just last week, he made some strange egg tacos and put them on Facebook[3]; his own invention!

Bobby and Christian and Christian and Hannah remained best friends for life. Christian is so loved by all four of his nephews, and he loved each and every one of them in a special way! It was like he was another dad to each of them. The night he went to be with our Lord, Noah

---

[3]   Facebook is a registered trademark of Facebook, Inc.

(Hannah's two-year-old) attacked Christian with a single shot NERF[TM4] gun. Christian said, "All right, little man, wait here." Christian went upstairs and came down with his semi-automatic NERF[TM5] gun and shot the snot out of Noah. Noah loved every minute of it.

Christian's last day on earth was fulfilling. He went hunting in Holy Jim Canyon and did a little exploring. He found this strange rock formation (see the table), took pics of it, and sent them to Bobby. He was trying to figure out what it was. I could go on all day about this awesome friend of mine, but I am out of time. I want to let Hannah speak.

Please join me in welcoming my daughter and her tank missionary, fresh out the Orange County Women's Central Jail, Hannah Mitchell.

By Hannah Mitchell, June 25, 2014

On Friday, June 13th, as I was gathering my things for class at the Orange County Women's Central Jail, a strange, disturbing feeling overcame me. It was a heavy, perplexed feeling, weighing down on my heart, so sudden and unexplainable. I told my bunkie about my bad feeling as it was starting to make me sick with worry, fear, and sadness, afraid with no explanation. She asked if I felt like something bad was going to happen. I replied, "I don't know; I think so." Eventually, the feeling disappeared. This affected me so much that I actually mentioned it to a few other people. Exactly five days later was my brother's last day with us here on earth.

The day after I received the news, I confided in the Lord and in my Bible. In the back of my Bible is a scripture to read for each day of the year. Curious, I looked up the scripture for June 18th. Daniel 4:1-4 was the passage:

> King Nebuchadnezzar, to the nations and peoples of
> every language, who live in all the earth: May you prosper
> greatly! It is my pleasure to tell you about the miraculous

---

4   NERF is a toy brand of Parker Brothers and a registered trademark of Hasbro.
5   Ibid.

signs and wonders that the Most High God has performed for me. How great are his signs, how mighty his wonders! His kingdom is an eternal kingdom; his dominion endures from generation to generation. I, Nebuchadnezzar, was at home in my palace, contented and prosperous. I had a dream that made me afraid. As I was lying in bed, the images and visions that passed through my mind terrified me. So I commanded that all the wise men of Babylon be brought before me to interpret the dream for me. When the magicians, enchanters, astrologers and diviners came, I told them the dream, but they could not interpret it for me. N.I.V.

Now I realize I am not Nebuchadnezzar, nor am I calling the Orange County Jail my palace in which I flourish, or my bunkie and fellow inmates wise men, but I now realize God's signs, God's wonders He attempted to reveal to me, though I could not make out what my feeling meant at the time, that God was warning me, preparing me for the death of my brother. Matthew 5.4 says, "Blessed are those who mourn, for they will be comforted." N.I.V. And I share this with you to hopefully comfort you as it comforts me. The Bible may say we shall not be the ones to determine our own fate, but Romans 3:28 also states that "we are made right with God by placing our faith I Jesus Christ and this is true for everyone who believes, no matter who we are." N.L.T. There is no doubt in my mind that Christian is in heaven now, watching over us all. Jesus said in John 214:2-4

My Father's house has many rooms; if that were not so, would I have told you that I am going there to prepare a place for you? And if I go and prepare a place for you, I will come back and take you to be with me that you also may be where I am. You know the way to the place where I am going." N.I.V.

The Lord wanted Christian. As great of a person as he was, who wouldn't? There is no event in our lives God hasn't already planned. On June 18,

2014, the Lord was ready and a room was prepared and waiting for Christian in heaven.

Proverbs 17:17 says, "A friend is always loyal, and a brother is born to help in a time of need." N.L.T. When I read this, it touched my heart. During the last three months of my incarceration, my brother and I became extremely close. There were a few times I became overwhelmed with everything that was going on in my life, and I'd take it out on my parents over the phone, and they'd pass the phone to Christian, not wanting to deal with any more of my craziness. Christian made me laugh and calmed me down every time. He wrote me letters almost every week, asking how I liked the sack nasty's, telling me how much he hates jail food and for me not to eat it. He even sent me a recipe for pruno (jail-made alcohol). I imagine he looked it up on YouTube like he always did, and I have no idea how the deputies actually let me get mail with instructions to make contraband or plans for his illegal activity of smuggling fireworks from Tijuana for his favorite holiday coming up, but nonetheless, I looked forward to his letters and looked forward to reading them. Christian and I got closer than ever these last few months, which I happen to believe was also another part of God's preparation for me with this life-changing event.

Christian became my best friend during my incarceration as well as a father figure to my son. He was an amazing brother, son, nephew, uncle, and friend whom we were all blessed to have in our lives, and I look forward to being reunited with him once again in heaven. I just thank the Lord that he gave me such a beautiful twenty-three years with the brother friend I will cherish forever and never forget. I will love you forever, Christian. -- Hannah

BOBBY'S LETTER to CHRISTIAN. -- This is so hard for me to say; what do you really say? One thing I can tell you, and I know you already know this, but "oh how I miss you." The whole family does! You were my best friend and always there for me. I wish I could have been there for you. Every time I'll be teasing my kids, hanging out with Noah, fishing and blowing something up in the desert, it will be with you in my thoughts, prayers, and heart. I love you Christian and always will. -- Bobby

GUEST SPEAKER: Bron Draganov -- A

Remembrance of Christian Mitchell 6/25/14 -- When my son died, I had a close old friend tell me that there was nothing he could say. When the young son of a physician friend of mine died recently, he told me that of all the people who had offered condolences, he met only with me, in order to hear somehow how to stem the loss. I'm not sure what good I was, but I can tell you that when terrible things like this happen, there is comfort in having people around you, who know you and who love you -- not to say anything, but to offer the support one gets just by being there. I thank all of you for coming today to support Bob and Angie Mitchell, and their family -- my friends. All of you know the loving family that they are -- that they've always been -- and it is difficult to hear of the problems they have had, and particularly difficult to know that Christian, a boy whom we all knew, who was always respectful and friendly, is gone.

I knew Christian growing up in local Boy Scout Troop 636. He and his brother were quite independent -- far more so than most boys their age. He and Bobby made Eagle quickly with little intervention by adult leaders. They knew what they wanted and they achieved it independently. They were naturals as Scouts. I think I was first drawn to the Mitchell boys when I saw Bob and Angie let their boys be boys growing up. As different from many of this generation, they allowed their boys to climb trees, rides motorcycles, shoot off fireworks, as I did with my boys because that's what I did when I was a boy.

They allowed their boys to get hurt and to learn from their experiences. I was drawn to Christian in particular because he was a natural at fishing, and loved to fish, just like my son. For those of you who know fishing, it takes a special knack to jerk the bait or lure just right so the fish is fooled.

And so, Bob and I took our youngest boys to Alaska together in 2002 to fish a mile-long wilderness lake for trout where not another sole could be seen, and for a whole week! The boys were in their element that week -- fishing rain or shine, always fishing. And when Christian had the personal record for the biggest fish that week dashed by my catching one bigger toward the end of our stay, the boys laughed and laughed as I pulled that fish aboard. Looking back, it was the best of times. It was a truly magical week of constant fishing and listening to old "Gunsmoke" radio tapes at night. It was a week that neither of the boys would ever forget and, in fact, Christian did a school project highlighting his week in Alaska with us. But it was also the last time that Christian and my son would spend on that lake. Since then, I had stayed in contact with the Mitchells and we would shoot every so often -- something that we all also had a common interest in.

Christian, just like his brother, was always a superb host to my boys and to the Scouts who participated in some of these shooting events. Just two months ago, we shot out in the desert, and lo and behold, Christian finally whipped me at trap shooting, and who would know then that the last time he competed with me, he'd win!

When I had dinner with the Mitchell boys at a local hangout a few months ago, there was no hint of any problems. And so, Christian's death came as a shock to me. I think these kinds of deaths always come as a shock. We never really know what's around the corner. It is very difficult for any of us to really know the depths of depression that ruin young lives.

We are here to celebrate Christian but also to provide support to Bob and Angie. When this happened to me, it felt like I was being crushed, like all the wind had been taken from my sails. I couldn't believe I would never see or speak with my son again. In a world in which most things are never final, this was as close to a final event I had ever had to deal with. I hadn't cried in thirty years, but as the death took hold, I began to cry. I will tell you that I have known a number of people who have lost children. Some get along but many do not. Those who do not have had no outside interests, no extracurricular activities, perhaps no work. They linger and never move on. I come from experience. I want to let you know, Bob and Angie, that life goes on eventually if you can take the right approach. I am here to tell you that you aren't the only ones who have lost children. I am here to tell you that the wind will come back in your sails over time, that you will find happiness again, and that a new normal will set in and follow you for the rest of your days. Best of all, I will tell you that you will remember Christian in the very best way for all that was good about him and, though you will miss him every single day and will always feel the loss, you will be able to move on despite the loss. It will never be the same, but it will be different and, if you handle it right by being busy, always busy, you will come out of this ok and see the light at the end of a long tunnel. I promise. We all love you. -- Bron Draganov

Appendix 3

At one point, before I started the book, I created the table below to track the emotional events Angie and I incurred in just one month. After the first month of tracking this information, however, it became too depressing to continue but I did switch to start writing this book.

February 29	Hannah cannot be found.
March 03	Hannah is back home with us
March 06	Hannah says she is going out with a new girlfriend and sleeping over.
March 07	Hannah's bedroom is a disaster. Noah's toys are all over the garage, and my workbench is covered with makeup and fingernail polish.
March 08	Christian says he's going out and staying at a guy friend's house. His computer is left on, two large wine bottles on his bedroom floor, a full wine class on his computer desk, bed is a mess, lights and TV on.
March 09	Christian comes home at 0600. Spends the day at the house working on fishing poles. Leaves to go fishing and states he may stay at a friend's house. Lost track of Christian again. Won't answer calls or text messages.
March 09	Angie and I confront Hannah for not contacting us to tell us she is safe, etc. The discussion is confrontational.
March 09	Bethany calls in the evening. Tells Angie that Bobby just had a serious injury.
March 14	Bobby suffers from his injury.

March 15	Bobby is harassed by some police at a gas station for an unstated reason.
March 16	A nice quiet Sunday.
March 30	Hannah arrested and not able to communicate with us. Bobby's wedding today.
April 02	I got an attorney to look into it. Hannah is charged with two counts of ADW with an attempt to inflict great bodily injury using her car, felony abuse of an elderly person, property damage, child abuse and endangerment, and driving while under the influence of alcohol and drugs with blood alcohol in excess of .08.
April 02	Noah is temporarily awarded to our custody while Hannah is in jail
April 03	Hannah finally gets to call us. She's been stored away stark naked for three days in a monitoring cell. Sounded so sad and demoralized. I wonder why Angie and I are so tormented with daily problems like these and after sixteen years we keep thinking it will end.
April 04	Hannah could not have her pretrial hearing due to her Public Defender on vac. There is a conflict, as her PD is defending one of Hannah's accusers in another case. PD is changed to another.
April 10	Hannah had to fight off a girl in jail to prove she will defend herself.
April 11	Angie and I visited Hannah. She is settling in to the jail life. I am very concerned about her. A motorcycle hit Christian as he was walking across the street in the crosswalk at 11:00 p.m. The motorcyclist ran and Christian suffered a severed rib at the spine. He's in horrible pain and scared the doctors will get him back on opiates. I completed the assembly of a table of argument s for Hannah's public defender.

ABOUT THE AUTHOR

Robert L. (Bob) Mitchell is a vice president of quality assurance and regulatory affairs for a major medical device company in Orange County, California. Along with his wife of thirty-two years, he raised three children in a solid Christian home, each of whom experimented with and were addicted to drugs for a time. Bob now has two children and four grandchildren.

Bob and his wife Angie were always involved in church and both of their boys achieved the rank of Eagle Scout. This story is evidence of how drugs and addiction know no boundaries. It could be your story. Bob prays that it is not.

Printed in the United States
By Bookmasters